PIGS IN CLOVER

A drunken misunderstanding changes Simon's life forever. Along with his wife and Great Dane, he moves to the wilds of Devon and takes up the challenge of leaving city life behind. Suddenly surrounded by pigs, chickens, goats and geese, it becomes a journey full of surprises — some funny, some tragic — leading Simon to question Mother Nature, himself, the food he eats, and his place in it all. Whether chasing turkeys, musing over life with the General (the resident alpha pig) or getting knee-deep in mud and mess, Simon learns what it takes to truly survive self-sufficiency and enjoy a slice of the good life.

PIGS IN CLOVER

OR, HOW I ACCIDENTALLY FELL IN LOVE WITH THE GOOD LIFE

SIMON DAWSON

ISIS
LARGE
PRINT

First published in Great Britain 2015
by
Orion
an imprint of the Orion Publishing Group Ltd.

First Isis Edition
published 2016
by arrangement with
the Orion Publishing Group Ltd.

A catalogue record for this book is available
from the British Library.

ISBN 978–1–78541–144–1 (hb)
ISBN 978–1–78541–150–2 (pb)

Published by
F. A. Thorpe (Publishing)
Anstey, Leicestershire

Set by Words & Graphics Ltd.
Anstey, Leicestershire
Printed and bound in Great Britain by
T. J. International Ltd., Padstow, Cornwall

For Debbie, what an amazing ride life's
turned out to be!

And for friends who shared some of the twists
and turns, Deacon and Darcy, Kylie and the
beautiful Bobby (Roberta's Pride).
Rainbow Bridge, guys, Rainbow Bridge. . .

CHAPTER
ONE

As of this moment in time, this very second, nobody has died, nobody has given birth, and nobody has escaped.

That's good.

The variations on a bad day are endless. I know, I've panicked my way through any number of them, charging, wellies flapping through the forecourt of the local petrol station in close pursuit of a small band of hideously evil, six-week-old piglets, in the vain hope of cutting them off before they reach the post office, which, for some God-known reason, always seems to be their goal.

Hooligans. All piglets are hooligans. They are. They may look cute and squidgy, but as soon as they're out of sight of mum, it's fags and booze all the way.

The trick is not to let them get too far from mum in the first place. Not always easy when it's mum herself who's tossing them over the electric fence and egging them on to go walkabout.

All the sows do it. Even Kylie, the matriarch. They seem to reach a point and think, I've had enough now. They were quite nice when they were little, but I think

I want a little "me" time for a while, and then they send their babies off on day trips.

Today, everything is fine. Everyone is where they should be. All 57 pigs, 18 sheep, 46 chickens, two ducks, one turkey, two geese (the terrorists of the chicken field), two wild cats, Niko and Morris, a Great Dane called Darcy, Dex, the one-eyed sheepdog, two horses, four goslings and two hand-milking goats.

All where they should be. But it wasn't always like this.

Ten years earlier . . .

"I want to give up work and move down here to Exmoor," Debbie shouted into the din.

"Yes," I nodded. I had absolutely no idea what she'd just said, but I didn't want to spend the entire New Year's Eve party yelling back at her, "Pardon? What?" and "Sorry?", so I'd been watching her eyes and judging whether I should be answering yes or no to what she was saying. I seemed to be doing rather well.

"Are you sure? I was worried you might not like it down here, it's so different from London," she yelled. London! I could lip-read that. At last, safe territory.

"Oh yes!" I said with some enthusiasm, chugging the last of my beer. We were in an Exmoor pub packed shoulder to shoulder with slightly grubby outdoor types and farmers who'd dressed up for the occasion by changing the strand of coloured string holding up their trousers. These were men of action, and I imagined if the call "My cows are loose" went up, they'd be only too delighted to form a scrum at the door in their eagerness to get out and do some rounding up. Except for the ones who would change their string back first — it would be a shame to dirty a new bit of twine.

There was a jazz band playing loudly in the corner with a singer who looked so old I wondered if the rest of the band had borrowed her from the local nursing home just to make up the numbers.

"I'm serious," Debbie said. "I'm burnt out at work. I want out, out of London. I didn't mean for all this to come out tonight, I'm so sorry, but I've had it with the whole 'work until you drop' thing. I can't do it anymore. I just can't. I really need out. I've been so scared of telling you — but we'll only do it if you're certain. Absolutely certain. Absolutely. Certain. *Are* you certain?"

Some of the farmers around us were waltzing, some jiving, some doing the twist. They were happy.

I was nearly at the end of my Exmoor Rein Beer and tilted the glass, smiling. It was pointless trying to speak; I still couldn't hear a word of what she was saying, but hoped it was something about the need for another drink. "Of course," I said.

Her chin dropped, and she mouthed the word, "Really?"

It was New Year's Eve, my glass was empty and I wanted another. I nodded enthusiastically, mouthing back, "Yes, really," delighted she seemed so pleased at my intention to drink the bar dry.

She got up and flung her arms around my neck, kissing me wildly and shouting, "I love you, I love you, I love you," into my ear. Then she picked up my glass and rushed for the bar, darting between the dancers. The band was still playing, though not necessarily all the same tune, and I was happy to see the singer still on her feet. I'm sure at one point I heard her shout into the microphone, "Do you know how old I am?"

I settled back into my seat, Debbie at the bar collecting our drinks, content that I was the relationship god.

The next day started badly. You know if you break a mirror it's said to be seven years' bad luck, or if you cry on your birthday you're said to cry for the whole 12 months until it's your birthday again, or if it rains on St Swithun's Day, it'll rain for 40 days and 40 nights. Well, there isn't an equivalent for New Year. If you ask me, there should be. Something like: if you agree to change everything about your life on New Year's Eve, your New Year's Day hangover will be the worst since records began, and it won't get any better when you sober up. That would work.

My hangover was the worst since records began, which, considering I was 32 years old and started drinking somewhere in my late teens, meant records began about 14 years ago. Put another way, it was the worst hangover ever.

"How much did I drink last night?" I said through furry teeth.

"It doesn't matter," Debbie said, bouncing onto the bed with both knees. "We were celebrating. Isn't it wonderful?"

It matters to me, I thought, but said, "What's wonderful?"

"Oh you," she punched me on the arm. "You know. Moving to Exmoor. We'll get the most beautiful little country cottage with some chickens in the back garden, and you can collect the eggs in the mornings, and I'll cook them for your breakfast. It'll be such bliss."

"Huh?"

"I've got it all worked out. I'll quit my job as soon as we get back . . ."

"*Huh?*"

". . . which won't be a hardship. Oh, Simon, I've been so unhappy."

I rummaged around inside my mind for some of the less sozzled brain cells, found half a dozen and strung them together as a basis of reasonable thought. Unfortunately, the mouth they had to project their ideas through was still a bit pissed.

"Quit work and move down here?" I stammered.

She bounced off the bed. "It all just came out last night," she said, folding clothes and tidying up the bedroom without looking back at me. "I shouldn't have started talking about it; I don't know why I did, not on New Year's Eve. But once I started, I couldn't stop." She stopped folding and shrugged. "Now you know everything. You're not disappointed, are you?"

She still didn't look around. I had the same feeling you get when you start watching a film halfway through.

"'Course not. No, no, no. No! Um, disappointed about what, exactly?"

"About me."

I think I'd liked to have sat up, but my head felt as though someone had concreted the space where my brain should be, and my mouth had that morning-after-a-kebab sensation, even though I hadn't had one. So I stayed where I was, which was flat on the bed.

"Don't be silly," I said. I could hear a stream running outside, and it reminded me that I hadn't been to the loo since I woke up, but I didn't have the energy to move. I started piecing snippets together. "So, you're unhappy at work?"

"Desperately."

"You want to resign and give up your career?"

"The world will probably survive with one less property solicitor," she said.

"And you want to sell up and move down here to Exmoor."

"Right. You haven't changed your mind, have you?"

Changed my mind? Boy, the beer must be strong down here, no wonder everyone looked so red faced. Had I really agreed to all this? I didn't want to leave London. I didn't want to leave my job. I *liked* my job. I liked my home. Why would I want to give it all up to live in a cottage and collect eggs?

"Of course, at first you would have to commute back and forth to work, which I know isn't ideal," Debbie chattered on. "Maybe see if you could do Monday to Thursday in London and then come home to Exmoor for long weekends. Please say you haven't changed your mind?"

The word that tattooed itself to the inside of my eyeballs so I could see its outline no matter where I looked was . . . retirement. I had horrific visions of buying a bungalow on the flat quite close to a parade of shops and a bus stop, chucking out all my Radiohead CDs and replacing them with compilations with "Chill" in the title, drinking tea — smelling of tea! — taking up golf and collecting bloody eggs. Why eggs? Don't they sell them in the shops down here? Is there an egg shortage in the West Country that the rest of us don't know about? Haven't they heard of a sup-er-mark-et? Who retires at 32 anyway? Career-wise I was only just getting into my stride, like a finely tuned athlete opening up down the back straight of the first lap, all muscles pounding . . . honed to perfection . . . athletic . . .

As estate agents, we see ourselves differently from the way the rest of the world sees us. We are, in fact, Adonises of the business world — just few recognise it. One day, there'll be an uprising or, better still, a strike. You think the country grinds to a halt when the underground and train drivers refuse to work? Imagine the chaos if in place of a board outside every estate agent's office in every high street up and down the country, there was one of those bins in which you burn wooden pallets, and we'd all stand around it, in our suits and with our gelled spiky hair, waving our Porsche and Mini key rings in the air and yelling "Scab" at passing solicitors, and we'd have Sarah Beenie as our spokesperson, "They want the recognition they deserve,

7

and until they get it, they're refusing to do any more accompanied viewings."

Could I really give all that up and move to the country? Try as I might, I couldn't imagine myself living anywhere but a major city centre. Which raised a problem: what to do about Debbie? I buried myself further under the quilt, which is as good as any way of avoiding a scene, at least until I was a little more sober. I watched her walk out with her head down.

Since when had communication between us dwindled so low that she didn't feel she could tell me she was unhappy, to the point that it all came flooding out at a New Year's Eve party? That's terrible. I wish I'd heard what she said. I could hardly admit that I hadn't caught a word of it, that her heart-to-heart had been drowned out by an OAP jazz singer and a bunch of whooping, ballroom-dancing farmers. To make matters worse, now she'd got it out of her system, she hadn't wanted to go over it all again, which left me colouring in an awful lot of blank space.

Bit by bit I got out of bed, washed, dressed and found her downstairs sitting at the table making lists. She'd dug out some paper and a pen from one of the drawers and spread them out. I poured myself a glass of water and sat down beside her.

Of course I could argue and inject some realism into her absurd notion of quitting everything we knew and understood and had worked for. Quitting all our friends and family. Our careers. Our home. I could burst her bubble in a trice and get us back to London and into our old routine, but it wouldn't be our old life again.

Not the way it had been. Not anymore. Too much had been said, too much had been confessed, and, in a way, it didn't matter that I hadn't heard it — what mattered was that she'd said it. She'd felt it, and she'd said it, and now it was impossible to ignore.

She'd be unhappy and would try and hide it, which would only make things worse. Besides, if she'd been that sad before, maybe things weren't the way I'd thought they were. And if things weren't the way I'd thought they were, then maybe we didn't want them back that way anyway?

She had stopped writing and was just staring at the paper, waiting for me to speak. I reached out and stroked her arm. I still felt horribly hung over.

"Show me how it could work," I said.

CHAPTER TWO

When the vendors of a property are themselves an estate agent and a solicitor, you'd be amazed how smooth and quick a transaction can be. Less than three months later and our trendy London flat was sold. It wasn't so bad, handing over the keys and a card with "Good luck in your new home" scrawled inside to the new owner, a pianist who fell in love with the high Victorian ceilings and said the acoustics would make him sound amazing.

"How do you feel?" I said. Debbie was scrunched up on half the passenger seat hugging a box of cooking equipment and a Le Creuset. The rest of the car was heaving under the weight of all our possessions, which mostly consisted of hundreds of books. Not to forget a Great Dane dog who'd sort of been folded into a gap at the back.

"I think I'm okay. I was just thinking how long we've been in that flat, thinking about work and about leaving and if we've done the right thing. You know, stuff."

Stuff. Oh great, you're thinking about stuff. Isn't it a little late to be doing that, considering we're hurtling down the M3 towards the land of no eggs, having given up a cushy life in London and now you're wondering if we've done the right thing?

"Not that I think we're doing the wrong thing."

That's nice to know.

"It's just, I wonder if I'll miss it?"

The glimmer of doubt, like the hint of a beautiful sunrise just as it begins to get light. Yes, Debbie had quit her job, and yes, we'd sold our home, but we were only going to rent in Devon, so, in theory, if it all went horribly wrong, we could move back and pick up the pieces of our old life again. In the meantime, I would travel back to work and live in London Monday to Thursday. I'd somewhat come round to the idea of having a pad in the country to come home to at weekends. It felt very . . . civilised, very Jane Austen, "*A house in London, a house in the country and ten thousand a year! Ten thousand a year, Mr Bennett!*"

The house in London was a room in my mother's place, and we'd probably need a touch more than ten thousand a year, but even so. It was one thing moving out for a less stressful, less hectic way of life, but you still had to pay your bills.

"Do you think you will? Miss it, I mean?" I said, smothering the words so they wouldn't betray any sign of hopefulness.

"No. Maybe a bit, but not enough to change my mind. Sorry."

Since "That Night", we'd made a pact to be honest and open with each other. I'd told her I wasn't keen on the move and I wasn't sure it would work, but I wanted her to be happy and we'd give it a try. If she wanted to.

11

Really wanted to. Really felt convinced it was the right thing for us to do. To, you know, get it out of her system. In return, she told me she knew it would work, that we'd be blissfully happy and it would be the best thing we'd ever done, I'd see.

Once we reached Devon, the first thing we did was search for somewhere to live. That meant visiting an estate agent. On the first day, we went to see a small house.

"I can't see the garden," I hissed to Debbie.

"There isn't a garden," the letting agent said, overhearing. I would never have answered someone else's question when I was on a viewing. That's *so* rude. I waved at her back and made a face at Debbie, who laughed. The agent didn't notice.

"Two bedrooms and a bathroom upstairs, lounge, big kitchen diner, vestibule and small study downstairs. No garden," she said. "Have you got pets?"

"A dog, but he's well behaved and never left alone, he's always with us," Debbie said.

"I see. Is he outside in your car?"

"Um . . . well, no, actually he's back at the holiday cottage — so you say there's no garden, well, that's not a problem for us, is it, Simon?"

"Isn't it?"

"No, 'course not. I like it. Do you like it? I like it."

"It's very remote," I said, looking out the window at . . . green. "And green. Very green."

"Green is good," Debbie said, flashing an apologetic smile at the agent. "He's from London."

12

"Can we have a talk about it?" I said, spinning round to face both of them. At least Debbie made a stab at covering some of her disappointment, which is more than can be said for the agent.

Outside, the agent slammed her car door and roared off.

"Come on," I said, "Let's explore."

We were about five miles outside Lynton and Lynmouth along the north Devon coast, just at the point where Exmoor meets the sea, in a tiny village called Barbrook: population about 50 people and as many dogs. The house was up the side of a cliff that masqueraded as a hill simply because someone had put a ribbon of tarmac up it. It was that sheer that at some points, travelling up, you couldn't see the road over the bonnet of the car. Halfway up, the hill levelled off for about 100 metres, and that's where the house stood, sideways to the road. A long farmhouse split into two properties. The house available to rent was the one nearest the road. It had a fresh coat of magnolia paint on the outside, white double-glazed windows and doors, a farmyard out the back that belonged to the farmhouse and a parking spot at the front. The steep road leading to it was a single-track lane edged either side with high banks covered in grass and greenery, and bare wintry trees growing up out of the top of that so if you stood on tiptoe, you could see through into the green fields beyond.

"It might be quite dark and dingy in the summer when all the leaves are out," I said.

Debbie linked my arm and squeezed. "No, it wouldn't. It's so peaceful, so beautiful." We started walking further up the road.

"Is this what you envisaged then, your heavenly country cottage?"

She shot a glance over her shoulder. "It's not chocolate boxy, but it's quite pretty. I love where it is. And I love the way it feels so cozy inside, especially with that log burner in the lounge. I can imagine you . . ."

She was doing a lot of imagining, and just about all of it involved me. Right now, she was imagining me as something of a lumberjack, bringing piles of logs into the house with an axe slung over one shoulder and then spending a fun-filled evening feeding bits of wood into the flames. Presumably this was after I'd collected the eggs. It struck me that I'd never lit a fire in my life. Not once. Prior to this iffy turn of events, if I wanted to get warm, I'd turn up the central heating. Now it looked like I'd have to go out and chop down a tree. She was still happily imagining, having moved on to something about candles, oil lamps and the wood fire, romantic dinners and sport on the TV — I think that last bit was for me. How do you light a fire anyway? Matches, clearly. Newspaper? Wood? Coal? Petrol? Who knows?

We struggled up the hill to the top without the aid of additional oxygen, but once there I refused to rule out the need for helicopter rescue to get back down.

"There," Debbie said, sweeping her arm out at the scenery, "What do you see?"

14

"Ah, now, that is a lot of green," I said, still puffing from the exertion. I seemed to be substantially more unfit than Debbie (when did that happen?). Ignoring me, and with a huge air of drama, she announced, "*That* . . . is Exmoor. Go on, spot a house. Go on, just one, one incey-wincey little house . . ."

Obviously, I couldn't. It was just miles and miles and miles of empty moorland. I tried to look excited and amazed.

"I can't," I said. "There aren't any. Wow. Imagine the housing estate you could put up here! I know some developers who'd love this. What an opportunity."

She swiped me hard. "Simon!"

"Okay, okay."

She put her arms around me, and I hugged her back.

"Do you think you could be happy here?" she asked.

"You do," I said. It wasn't a question, but she nodded anyway. "How about we take the house for six months and see how it goes?"

She squeezed me tight, leaning over and resting her chin on my forehead (she's quite a bit taller than me).

"A year," she said. "We'd need to give it a year. Oh, and one more thing, would it be okay if I got a horse?"

I heaved her away. "Absolutely no way! No way. I'm not having a horse. You've got to be kidding! No way. Out of the question. No!"

CHAPTER
THREE

We got a horse. She's called Ima Georgie Girl — Ima being the breeder's prefix, so her brother is Ima Pukka Boy, and her sister Ima Maggie May — on account of the fact that she was born on St Georgie's day.

So. I'm 32, and now I own a horse. Thirty-two; not 14, or even 18, or even twenty-something. Thirty-two. I have a house in the country and a horse. Okay, they're not just mine, they're ours, but it's the same thing. I share the responsibility. When I'm home (notice that I now refer to this rented outpost as home, at least in front of Debbie, who had gone ballistic one Saturday afternoon claiming I wasn't trying to see it as our home), I want to muck in and be part of it all.

If car nuts are petrol-heads, is it correct to say horse nuts are hay-heads? If so, Debbie is one. She practically lived at the stables throughout the whole of her teenage years and right into her early 20s. She knows all about horses. The only thing I know is that the Superman actor Christopher Reeve fell off one, broke his neck and lived the rest of his life in a wheelchair. Sobering thought. I had no intention of ever getting on a horse. I especially had no intention of ever getting on Georgie Girl. Horses seem to come in bands or groups. At the bottom, you've got Bomb-proof, fully trustworthy in any situation. Then you've got Good-to-do, okay in most situations. Then it goes Scatty, which speaks for itself, then Flighty, a stage worse, then Murder, which, spelled backwards reads Red Rum, so you can guess that one, too. And right at the very top of the Naughty Equine Leader Board is Chestnut mare, which is like a fiery red-headed woman with permanent PMT: beautiful to look at but scary to be around. Georgie Girl is a chestnut mare. A thoroughbred cross Irish Draft chestnut mare.

"I'm not riding her," I said, peering over the stable door just as Georgie looked up and discharged two nostril-barrels of snot right into my face.

"No, she'd kill you," Debbie agreed, offering a sleeve to help mop up. "You need lessons first."

There was only one way I was ever going to have a lesson on a horse, and that was if Debbie bought a set for me, wrote it on a card, put the card in an envelope, wrapped the envelope in pretty wrapping paper with a heart drawn on one corner and gave it to me as a surprise present because she loved me. Which is what happened.

I groaned when I opened it.

If that wasn't bad enough, she talked me into getting a pair of jodhpurs, the stretchy horse-riding trousers that are so tight I looked like a chunky ballerina. I could have danced the *Nutcracker*, and very nearly did on my first lesson when I wore my customary boxer shorts underneath and trotted round, using my testicles as a bouncy cushion between me and the saddle. For two nights after, I had to sit on a packet of frozen peas. For the next lesson, I dug out an old jockstrap from my days of playing rugby. Rugby to horseback riding: where on earth had it all gone so wrong?

I don't know when I started enjoying it. You know when you're learning to drive a car and at some point you notice you've changed gear without consciously going through the procedure, and you think, wow, I'm really starting to become a driver. Well, at some point I asked for a canter just by thinking, "I think I'll canter now," and suddenly we were cantering. It was a beautiful moment, even for me. But it was an isolated beautiful moment. Most of the moments were soaked in pain and humiliation in front of huge-bottomed, huge-bosomed, bossy women who, presumably because of their frail sex (ha!) didn't want to get into the army and chose pony club instead, and would stand in the middle of the school yelling utterly unintelligible things, with me riding around the outside.

"Put your leg on! Put your bloody leg on, Simon! PUT, IT, ON!"

I'd look down, half expecting to see one of them had fallen off. It was all so confusing.

The Ying to Exmoor's Yang was London. London was safe, didn't involve a change of underwear style and rarely had bossy women shouting at me. You know where you stand in London, or, more accurately, as an estate agent you know where you sit, which is in a lovely big seat behind a great big desk.

There's nothing like a big desk. I leant back in my sumptuous leather chair, stroked my tie straight over the crisp, white business shirt and glanced once more at the ordered, tidy, composed desk top in front of me. The telephone was spotless and had these cool blue lights that flashed when it rang, and the ring tone wouldn't have sounded out of place in a stockbroker's million-pound apartment. Next to the telephone was a writing pad with notes and messages in neat handwriting numbered 1 to 27 down the page. Number 28 was waiting to be added.

I was in London. At work. Where I belonged. A place where nobody I knew talked about chickens — by the way, I'd discovered they do sell eggs in Devon. They sell loads of them. If anything, the county is awash with eggs. If they weren't so round, they could make mountains with them.

My mobile trilled. "Guess what?" Debbie asked.

"What am I guessing?" I said, holding the phone to my ear, aware that others in the office were pretending not to listen. One was even humming, though not too loud, as then he really wouldn't have been able to hear.

"I've got a job," Debbie announced.

I sprang forward. "Really? That's great. Debbie, honestly, that's great. I didn't even know you were looking. Since when did you start looking? It doesn't matter. I'm so proud of you, well done! When do you start? How about I buy you a couple of skirt suits from here? The shops are so dowdy in Devon compared with London. A couple of blouses — I know you can't try them on, but I know your size. Oh, Debbie, that's fantastic!"

"It's not as a solicitor. It's not in an office at all," she said.

Oh.

"I met this lady in the lane when I was out with the dog. She's got a riding centre just up from us that does residential horse-riding holidays for adults. Advanced trekking across Exmoor, that sort of thing. She needs a cook. She asked me if I'd be interested, and I said yes."

"You want to be a cook?"

"Why not? I don't want to be a solicitor anymore, and I've got to do something."

"But a cook?"

"Breakfast in the morning, vegetarian or full English. A lay-and-leave lunch, like a small buffet, and a two-course evening meal for between six and 14 people. The budget I'd have to work with is tight, but I'm getting quite good at being thrifty these days. I think I'd enjoy it."

"You don't want to be a solicitor anymore? Not . . . anymore?"

"Simon, you know I don't. What did you think, that I'd get bored and go back to work in a local solicitor's practice and before I know it end up back in London? Oh, of course, that's it. That's what you thought would happen, isn't it?"

It had, um, maybe crossed my mind.

"No, 'course not," I lied.

"This is our life now. Devon. Exmoor. Here. Not London. I know it's tough at the moment what with you spending so much time commuting back and forth, but it won't always be like this. I'm not going back to

London, I'm not going back to work as a solicitor, that's in the past now. And I'm sure you won't be going back to London for much longer either. I've been thinking and working stuff out, and I've got some ideas."

I looked at the guys in the office and did a pantomime shrug that said, "Women, huh!" I had this vision of Debbie in the lounge, the fire crackling with red and orange and yellow flames in the corner. Our sofas hadn't gone with the décor and feel of the place, so we'd bought two cheap and cheerful king-size quilts and quilt covers that did match and used them as throws, adding big, overstuffed cushions, making it all comfortable, and shuffled the sofas right up close huddling the fire. I imagined Debbie huddled close to the fire, too, if she could get past the dog who'd decided on day one the warmest spot was his. It's hard not to huddle close to the fire, even when you're not cold. I looked out of the office window at the grey London high street, the grey shop fronts, the grey road, the grey pavements and the grey people bustling by, and thought there are just as many shades of grey outside my window as there are shades of green outside hers.

"I'm not sure that's appropriate," I said, which was code for I DON'T WANT TO LEAVE LONDON! I was sure she'd pick up on it. She didn't.

"There are lots of things we can do down here to save money, and the more money we can save, the less time you'll have to spend working in London. Plus, now I've got a job."

None of this was making me want to jump for joy.

"Her name is Steph," Debbie said.

"Whose name is Steph?"

"My new employer, silly. I'm going up tomorrow morning and she's going to show me what's what around her kitchen. Then we're going to look at buying some chickens. Steph said that it would be nice if we had fresh eggs to cook for the guests each day."

"We're not getting any chickens, though, are we?"

"No. We haven't got anywhere to put them, we haven't even got a garden."

"Debbie!"

"We probably won't even buy any, we're just going to look."

"Debbie!"

"It's totally impractical, totally out of the question for us to have any at home. I know that, I'm not stupid."

Yeah, that's the problem.

"Promise me you won't buy us any chickens," I said.

"Don't be silly. I don't need to promise. You can trust me, you know that."

The next time I went home, Debbie said she had a surprise for me. You won't need to sit down for this. You won't need a cup of sweet tea ready for the shock, either. We had chickens.

"You said it was totally impractical and out of the question," I stammered.

"Yes, to have chickens at home. We're not having them at home. We're keeping them at Steph's in return for looking after all her chickens, too."

"You promised. You said I could trust you."

"I said you could trust me that it was totally out of the question for us to have any at home, and we haven't. We've got them at Steph's."

I knew I should never have married a lawyer.

I slumped down on the second best seat in the lounge. The dog, a sensitive little soul who had recognised the magnitude of my return after five days away and concluded that nothing short of a wall-of-death welcome was in order, had careered around the lounge at full speed, launching himself across from sofa to sofa without ever once touching the floor — pretty impressive for a 12-stone Great Dane — until after 20 laps he had flopped down, exhausted, in the best spot, happy I'd been properly greeted. When he was calm, we straightened up the room, and Debbie gave me a long glass of wine and an even longer kiss.

"I know you've been against chickens, but when you see them, you'll fall instantly in love," she said.

"I don't want to fall in love with a chicken. I don't want to fall in love with anything."

The dog yawned loudly.

"Except you," I said, lying down next to him; Great Danes are brilliant cuddlers. Burying my face in his neck, I said, "I don't know anything about chickens. This is all your thing, not mine."

Debbie was perched on the arm of the sofa beside me.

"Are you really annoyed?" she said.

"A bit. I feel like everything's running away down here and I don't belong to any of it. You've got chickens and a horse, a home, a job and friends here — I can't believe how quickly you've become part of it all. A few months ago you were a solicitor in an office. Now look at you."

She stared into her wine. "Remember when we met and you told me you were a cat person and detested all dogs?" I undid myself from the cuddle with the dog and sat up.

"That's not the same thing," I said.

"It kind of is. I've always loved all animals, so I know it's easier for me, but I don't do any of these things without really thinking them through first. You only thought you didn't love dogs because you'd never got close to one."

"So as soon as I spend any time around chickens, you believe we're going to be best friends forever?"

"You didn't think you were going to like Georgie. She rides better for you than she does for me."

"She's still your horse — I know she's ours," I said, cutting her off before she had a chance to interrupt. "But she'll always be more yours than mine."

"Mm, maybe — perhaps we'll look at that. The point is, all of these things are for us, to give us a better life, and just because you haven't had them in the past doesn't mean you won't love them in the future."

"Why does that sound like a threat?"

"Because that's how you've decided to take it, even though that's not how it was meant."

The house had that smoky, open-fire smell and did feel cozy with the flames flickering in the corner, and I kind of got the fact that it's not quite the same cuddling with the one you love in front of a radiator. But it just felt . . . I want to say old-fashioned, but that's not the right word, because old-fashioned makes you think of swirly carpets and wallpaper that my granddad would recognise from his boyhood, and it didn't have that. The décor was crisp, clean and neutral.

Maybe simpler is a better word. It felt simpler, less complicated than London houses with its sheepskin rugs on the floor, a small portable television in the corner, a couple of oil lamps glowing, some candles alight and the fire burning away.

"I just don't get this compulsive need for chickens," I said.

"Have you ever seen one?"

"Don't be horrible, of course I have."

"Not on the telly or a picture. Have you ever seen one live?"

She already knew the answer to that.

"You already know the answer to that," I said. "But I've never seen a death-watch beetle or a funnel-web spider either and I know I don't like them."

I was right: I didn't like the chickens.

I refused to smile when the cockerel, a huge red and orangey thing with a blood red comb sticking up out the top of his head, charged around bonking all the females.

"The hens can't stop the boys having sex with them, other than by running away, which is pretty ineffective in a small area like this," Debbie whispered. "But if she doesn't like the male . . . well, when he ejaculates, she

25

can fire the semen right back out of her and straight back into him."

I winced. "Blimey, that's going to ruin your day."

There were about 20 chickens in total. Only four were ours. As soon as we had our own chicken house, we'd be able to separate them from the others and have our own spot on Steph's land, as long as we continued to look after her chickens as payment.

The next weekend we went out and bought a chicken house. We also bought 55 metres of netting to set up around the house so they'd have a safe area in which to play because the netting could be electrified to keep out predators. We also had to buy the equipment to electrify the netting. Because the set-up was far away from the house, we needed a leisure battery to supply the electric current. And a battery charger to charge the battery when that ran dry. In all, we spent about 500 pounds.

We put the chickens in, and the next morning we got one egg. *One* egg. The going rate for eggs is a pound for half a dozen. For 500 pounds I could have bought 3,000 eggs. Yet despite that, I have to admit that it was an exciting moment reaching into the nest box and pulling out our first one. I tried hard not to show it, but I was thrilled.

"You're grinning," Debbie claimed.

"I'm not," I said, grinning.

We took it home and had half each, on toast. The colour, the taste . . . it was creamy and delicate and stunning. Whether it was worth 500 quid or not, I'm not sure, but it was seriously good.

As soon as the egg production started in earnest and we were getting two or three eggs every day, one hen went broody, sitting on a nest of eggs and refusing to budge. That meant that out of our three hens and one cockerel, a third of our egg-laying workforce was on maternity leave.

"Can't we stop it?" I said.

"Why? In a few weeks we'll have tiny baby chicks. You'll be a dad."

I beamed, then shut the beam off. "I told you I don't like chickens," I said.

I liked the eggs, I just didn't like the chickens. Stupid things, running over to me when I called them, and if I had a bucket of feed they'd go nuts. But I didn't like them. I'd watch them feed, pecking and scratching the ground, and afterwards they'd come over to me and if I was inside the netting they'd use me as a perch. One even fell asleep on my foot and I didn't move for a whole hour because I didn't want to wake her. Stupid things.

I called the broody hen Doris and only sat talking to her because that's what you do with women who are cooking babies. I thought she might be a bit lonely and need cheering up, so I told her about work. I think she liked it. One morning I was chatting to her, telling her about a particularly emotional house owner in the week who'd spent ages crying at me because she couldn't move home on the day she wanted, when I noticed movement under Doris. I ran and got Debbie, who was cleaning down the kitchen after a morning service.

"I think she's done it," I said excitedly.

We hurried back and found Doris off the nest. She wouldn't let us see the chicks that were hiding under her feathers like it was a long skirt, but we could hear them. Debbie checked the nest.

"There's one left," she said, pointing to the only whole egg among the empty shells. Carefully, she touched it. "It's still warm."

"Will Doris go back and sit on it?"

"Not now she's got off the nest."

"So what happens?"

She reached in and very carefully picked it up. From inside, the chick gave a soft cheep. Debbie shrugged. "Unless we can find somewhere warm quickly, somewhere with a constant temperature, it'll get cold and die before it has the chance to hatch."

"So put it somewhere warm," I said.

"Yeah, where?"

At home we didn't have an airing cupboard or radiators, and the fire got hot and cold depending how much wood you put on it. "The oven?" I said.

Debbie frowned a no.

"The only place I can think of . . ." she said, tailing off. "It's a bit — oh, what the hell."

With that, she pulled the front of her top down and slipped the egg, the unborn chick still cheeping quietly inside, down the centre of her cleavage until it sat safe and snug to continue incubating between her bangers.

"Just remind me not to run anywhere," she said.

CHAPTER
FOUR

That evening was just weird. We sat in front of the fire picking names for a chick that was incubating between Debbie's boobs — Charlie if it was a boy, Ayla if it was a girl — as though this was a perfectly normal thing to do.

"If you start singing to it, I'm leaving you," I warned when she stroked the egg with the tips of two fingers. "I mean it, one verse of *Kumbaya, My Lord* and you won't see my bum for dust."

She started humming it. I began to get up and she grabbed my arm.

"I'm kidding, sit back down," she said. "Besides, you were the one who wanted to pick a name."

"I know, just don't go all freaky on me, okay? I don't want to be married to an earth mother. I want to be married to a normal, sensible woman."

"I am normal and sensible!"

"Debbie, you've got a chicken hatching between your boobs." We both looked down. That alone would have been bad enough, but there was more, so I embellished, "We've got the TV on mute so it can concentrate — like a chick needs to concentrate to hatch — the lights are low, there are candles everywhere . . ."

29

"I'm getting a nice birthing atmosphere going. It's nice."

"It's odd."

Actually, I couldn't work out if it was nice or odd. Or both. Can something be both? I took a sip of wine and would have sat back if the dog wasn't taking up far more than his fair share of the sofa, so I sat on the edge, elbows on knees.

Of course it was odd, but maybe not as odd as it would have been if we were in London. It's a strange thing that location can dictate the level of absurdity even when you're in the comfort of your own home and nobody else can see you. Which probably means I'm judging my life's weirdness by how I think the neighbours would react if they knew what I was doing. I'm not sure that's good. All the neighbours I've ever had were a bit strange themselves. Mind you, even in the wilds of Exmoor I can't see that people are going to think hatching a chicken between a woman's boobs is normal behaviour.

But I guess I did feel a little more comfortable than I would if we were somewhere else, somewhere more built-up, and I guess it does feel kind of nice. I'm not sure I can fully get to grips with the role of the expectant father, even if I do have the urge to pace the floor, but . . . it's exciting.

"I don't think it's going to be long now," Debbie said. "Are you excited even a little bit?"

"Oh yes," I said, mouthing a false yawn, for which I received a slap on the arm. Then the slap turned into a rub, and finally a stroke.

In the most girly, pink, feminine version of *Alien* ever, the chick was born. Actually it wasn't so much born as peeled, because after it made an initial hole, we helped by peeling bits of the shell away around it, as though we were unwrapping a live present.

"You're a dad," Debbie beamed at me, adding, "Can you get me a little hot water and a towel please?"

I laughed. Good one.

"Shush, not so loud, you'll scare her. Please, hot water and a towel?"

"Oh sorry, I thought you were kidding." I got up. "You're really not kidding? You really want —"

"— yes, I really want. Hurry up! I've got bits of shell and goo running down between my boobs."

With an, "Eerrr, yuck," I turned and rushed out.

I'm not squeamish, at least I don't think I am, though, in truth, it's never really been tested. I've never seen more blood than a single paper cut can amass. I've never had a child, so I haven't changed a nappy or been thrown up over. In fact, I've led a pretty goo-free life. Yet, however untested my level of squeamishness was, I was confident I could cope with the contents of an egg.

"Oh, my, God," I said, returning and handing Debbie the towel, one corner dipped in hot water. The chick was now completely out, and Debbie was holding it in her hand. It looked shattered, its head flopping about like it was about to nod off to sleep.

That wasn't the "Oh, my, God" bit though. The "Oh, my, God" bit was the trail of savage destruction wreaked across Debbie's chest. There were bits of shell stuck to her skin, blobs of blood, veins — veins! — and this mucus-like, clear snot trickling down. It was pretty disgusting.

"That's pretty disgusting," I said.

"Helpful," she said. "Here, can you take her?"

I didn't want to. "Do I have to?"

She gave me a look.

"Okay, I'll just go and scrub my hands first." I've seen *House*.

"No. Your hands are clean, just take her."

Other than run away, a thought that didn't seem a wholly bad idea in the circumstances, I didn't see I had much choice. So I held out my hand.

Debbie gave me the chick.

She felt . . . tiny. I know that's a rubbish description, but, honestly, that word sums up everything about her. Her eyes, her claws, her beak, her wings, the little feathers that were all slicked back, just so tiny. I could feel her little heart beating through my fingertips. She didn't feel slimy at all: she felt warm, and she smelled a bit like warm vanilla sick.

"You're grinning," Debbie said, dabbing and mopping at her chest and generally stirring all the bits into a big soup before scooping them into the towel with a final sweep. I had the chick cupped in my hands in front of me and, for an insane moment, had an urge to get the camera, take my top off and recreate that picture with the topless guy holding a newborn baby in his hands, only mine would be with a newborn chick.

"How do you know she's a girl?" I said.

Debbie rearranged her top. "I don't. You can't tell with chickens until they're a few weeks old."

"Oh. So why did we pick names then?"

"Well, she's got to be named at some point," she said, taking the chick from me and placing it in the bucket we had arranged with a deep soft bed of clean straw in the bottom. We snuggled her in and placed it under the worktop light in the kitchen to keep cozy, then wandered off to bed. It's amazing how tiring giving birth can be.

In the morning I was the first one up. I threw on a fleece and boxers and sneaked downstairs. "Good morning, my little baby girl," I said walking into the kitchen. "This is your daddy speaking, we met briefly last night. The other one there was your mummy — she's the one with the big boobies."

I tipped the bucket so I could see inside, expecting a little face to be looking up at me. She didn't look up. She lay there. Still. Looking deeply asleep. Or dead.

When someone's suspected of being dead, don't they put a mirror in front of their face to see if they're still breathing? I didn't have a mirror, though I guess at a push I could hold up the chick in front of the bathroom mirror . . .

In the end I poked her. She wasn't asleep. She was dead.

"Oh." I felt my eyes close. How could it have gone through all of that, all that growing inside the shell, developing into a perfect little chick, just to come out and die?

I made two coffees and took them up. Debbie was still snoozing. I put the mug beside her and sat on the bed. She must have guessed because she said, "She didn't make it, did she?"

"I'm sorry," I shook my head. "I don't understand. She was fine last night. How could she have gone through all of that and then right at the end when all she had to do was rest and recover, she dies?"

"Her mum would've known there was something wrong — her proper mum, not me. That's probably why she got off the nest and left her." She rubbed my arm. "We gave her every chance."

I've never had pets, so I've never had anything die on me before. This was my first experience. It's a real bugger.

I tried not to think about it until I got into the car later that day for the drive back to London. The trip takes about four and a half hours. I put on some heavy music and turned up the volume trying to fill myself with it so I didn't have to think. It didn't work, so I turned it off and let in the thoughts. I knew at some point this was going to happen, so I might as well get it over with.

Okay, look, I know it's just a chick, and I don't even like chickens. It's not like it's anything important. It's just . . . I don't know. It's just such a waste. Such a stupid waste. I bet it was a girl. I let my mind drift back to holding it, so tiny, so vulnerable. I remembered how warm she was, and I remembered that vanillary sick smell.

Stupid, stupid, stupid.

After a while I turned the music back on and set the volume not just high but all the way up. Then I put my foot down and sped though the lanes like a racing driver. It's just a stupid, stupid, stupid chick. A stupid, stupid chick. I thought about her all the way back.

I didn't tell any of them at work. London has this way of consuming you, so nothing outside seems to matter anyway. It's comforting in a strange way.

I dealt with people who wanted to buy a home and with people who wanted to sell a property — never the other way around — when I received a text message from Debbie: *How do you feel about getting pigs?*

I sent one back: *You do, you're dead!!!!!*

She sent one back to me: *I'm melting, aaahhhh!!!!!*

I sent one back to her: *You are a witch, too!!!!!*

We like to text with exclamations marks. It adds feeling.

It was hours before the office went quiet enough to call her.

"Pigs?" I said as soon as she answered.

"There's space at work in the corner of a field for a couple of pigs. I suggested to Steph that we should get two and have one each in return for you and me looking after them. When the time comes, she could turn hers into homemade sausages and bacon for her guests, and we could do the same for us. You'd have to build a house for them and make the area safe and secure, but I thought you'd enjoy doing that. If anyone knows about houses, you do."

"Yeah, I know how to sell them. I have no idea how to build them!" I could taste the panic in my mouth. It tasted coppery.

"It's just a big box made out of wood. You'll be able to do it easily."

"But it's got to have a roof on it. And a doorway. I've never done anything like that in my life. What makes you think I'd enjoy doing it?"

"Because you're creative and clever."

Normally I'm as shallow as the next man and will gobble up compliments like chocolate, but panic trumps vanity every time.

"I am not going to be drawn into an argument about building a house because we aren't going to be getting any pigs. I'm not creative. I'm not a pig keeper. I couldn't build a house if my life depended on it. We are not getting pigs. That's a step way too far, Debbie."

Silence. That coppery taste was now making my mouth water. Or was it the thought of chocolate?

"Debbie?"

"I'm here, you don't need to get hysterical. Or hyperventilate. Look, how about we go and have a look at them? You've never seen pigs before. We won't even take any money with us, and I'll tell the guy we're just going to see. It'll be something to do together. It'll be fun, and I promise we won't buy any."

No, it was definitely panic.

At the end of the week, I left work and drove home with a feeling that was becoming more familiar, a feeling of falling, of being out of control. I'd started dreaming of aircraft crashes, too. Every night in my sleep I'd board a plane and know that it wasn't going to make it, that it would climb up into the sky only to plunge headfirst down again. My subconscious is one of the unsubtle types. Short of one of my fellow passengers whacking me around the head with a sick bag while the plane was in freefall, yelling, "Your life is out of control and you're *dooooomed!*", it would be hard not to pick up on the message.

I pulled up outside the house and dragged my bag up the steps. I could smell the log fire and wondered if I could entice Debbie into making love in front of it as soon as the dog had gone to bed (I'm rubbish in front of an audience).

The door was unlocked and I pushed it open. Inside, standing there on the slate-tiled floor looking up at me was a small, black-and-white baby lamb. We didn't have a baby lamb. Did we?

I turned around and walked out, shutting the door behind me. Then I opened it again and peeked in. The lamb was still there. It baa'd at me.

I double-checked. I definitely had the right house, it was just the contents that were wrong. I dropped my bag outside and tried going in once more. The lamb seemed pleased. It baaa'd again. I had no idea what the protocol of meeting a lamb was: should I shake its foot or pet it? Hang on, maybe they bite, maybe they're dangerous — *I don't know, I've never met a lamb before!* You can't be too careful when confronted by a wild animal in your own vestibule. I didn't want to be bitten. So I crossed my arms.

That didn't make it happy. It took two steps forwards, bleated a long "Baaaaa" and, presumably irritated that I wasn't responding, jumped up and did a flying head butt at the soft, squidgy area between my legs.

CHAPTER
FIVE

I heard the door to the kitchen open and Debbie blurted out, "I'm sorry, please don't blame me, it really wasn't my fault. Someone knocked on the door and handed me the lamb — why are you bending over like that?"

"Balls," I croaked. "Lamb. Head butt. Balls."

"Oh no. Naughty lamb hurting daddy like that! Are you okay? He's hungry, it's what they do when they're hungry. He's searching for his mother's teat. I'll get him a bottle."

I stumbled past them both and flopped head first on the sofa. I only moved later to shift into a more appropriate position for an argument, and I did that gingerly. Once settled, I started. I accused her of everything from wrecking my life to wrecking our marriage. I told her that she was selfish, that she was wicked, cruel, insensitive, and I told her she was a bare-faced liar.

"You expect me to believe that someone knocked and said, 'Please can you take this lamb?'" I said. "Not in a million years. It doesn't happen. You got that lamb behind my back because you knew I'd say no."

39

In the middle of it, someone knocked on the door and said they'd heard we'd taken in a lamb, could we take in another as they'd just found one on the moor lying next to its dead mother?

"What the hell is this place?" I said when they'd left the lamb and driven away.

"It's what happens here," Debbie said.

I stomped about a bit, my hand carefully cupping my damaged bits, but I'd lost the energy for a fight. "Well, it doesn't change anything. We can't keep head-butting sheep in the house."

"No, I've arranged with Steph that they can have a stable until they're big enough, and then they can go into one of her fields. She wants to get half a dozen ewes anyway, so they can all live together."

"Well, that's all right then," I fumed, because I couldn't think of anything else to say, and went for a lie down.

I drank wine for the pain which made me melancholy. I felt sad for my old life, and I felt sad for my new life. And in much the same way I felt sad for my old wife and sad for this strange new person that had appeared inside the body of the old one like a Stepford wife in reverse.

I could hear her talking to the lambs as she fed them again. I felt everything I never wanted to feel towards her — unsupportive, uncommunicative, distant and just an arse. But equally, since when did this animal-loving farmer's wife appear? The girl I knew and fell in love with was a townie solicitor, not Little Bo Peep.

40

I finished the last glass in the bottle with a slurp. I hadn't eaten and felt light-headed. At least most of the pain had now gone. I wasn't sure I was up to lovemaking in front of the fire, but then I was pretty sure Debbie wouldn't want to anyway.

I felt bad for what I'd said. I really thought she'd gone out and got the lamb behind my back. She wasn't wicked or cruel or anything like that. She just had things she needed to do with her life, and she was determined to do them. She had a . . . I don't know . . . a vision of how she wanted our life to be. I'm still not certain if this vision is the reason for moving down here or the result of it. But she must have seen something in me that made her confident I'd fit in and be part of this Utopia, even happily be part of it.

Let me tell you there is nothing scarier than living with a woman who has a vision of a better life. Personally I'd be happy living in a city centre one street away from a 24-hour McDonalds with a bar and a coffee shop on either side of it, but there you go.

"I'm sorry," I said, standing behind her. "I didn't mean what I said. It's just . . . it's all so different down here, different from what I'm used to in London. I'm trying to get my head around it." I put out a hand and touched her shoulder. "You've got to admit it's a touch weird walking into your own home and getting a head butt in the goolies by a sheep!"

"I suppose," she said, but I could hear her smiling. She stood up, and I noticed the baby's bottle in either hand, the lambs still nosing around them in case there was a drop left. "So you don't think I'm a bitch, selfish, a liar, ruining your life and angling to split us up then? Did I miss anything?"

I looked down. "Did I really say all that? I'm sorry. But I had just been nutted by Larry there." I desperately wanted to talk about what we were doing, to work out if it was all a big mistake moving down and what we could do to rectify it, but now wasn't the time.

"You can't call him Larry, think of another name." She reached down and touched the lamb's head.

"Colin," I said. "We'll call him Colin."

I thought, so now we've got sheep, too. Chickens, chicks, a horse and now —

Debbie said, "Georgie, Colin and chickens."

"Pardon?"

"Or was it horse, sheep and chickens? That you were thinking?"

"You missed chicks," I said.

She nodded. "Makes it sound better. I bet when you were a kid you used to ask for your pocket money in pennies so it looked more. We're going to look at pigs tomorrow. We are not going to buy any, but we are going to look. After being so nasty to me tonight, you owe me. And you will do it with stunning good grace and smiles and you will not ruin the day, okay?"

"I was going to say exactly the same thing to you," I said.

"Good."

"Good."

Not good.

Apart from the whole animal thing, I was becoming aware that I don't really enjoy being outside. I've nothing against the nip from the house to the car, or the car into a shop, but any period longer than that and I start to feel . . . well, messy. The wind blows your hair, it's dusty and it's either too hot or too cold or it's raining. I don't mind riding out Georgie over the moor, but part of that is only because I love the feeling of getting back inside afterwards.

Now I have a weekend at home after a long week away at work, two days off, and I'm expected to go outside and look at stinky, dirty, no doubt loud and ugly pigs. Pigs! I'm a city boy, what do I want to go and look at a poxy pig for? Oink, oink, little porker, I shall think of bacon sandwiches the whole time I'm there.

"Can I have a fiver, please?" I asked the following day as we drove through the lanes towards the pigs.

"What for?"

"Ah-*ha*! You *do* have money on you! You promised you wouldn't so you couldn't be tempted. Hand it over . . ." I held out my hand.

"You silly arse," she said, smiling.

"I'm going to have the biggest bacon sandwich in the world when I get home," I said.

"You said you'd be nice."

"I *am* being nice. This is what I do when I'm being nice. Big smile, see?" I pointed at my face.

"Next left, and we're looking for Single Oak Farm," Debbie said.

"Very original. No guesses where they got that name from."

"Says the man who called his lamb Colin. There!"

I braked and turned in. The yard was gravel and dirt and contained a jumble sale of dead, dying and decomposing caravans, dozens of them. Negotiating a path between them, a short man with an enormous belly waddled towards us, a once clean T-shirt stretched so tight across his front you could see the dip of his belly button. As he drew closer, he hoiked up his jeans. The jeans and the T-shirt didn't meet.

We got out of the car.

"Hello, hello, hello, hello," he said, his big round face alive with the most infectious smile I've ever seen. I grinned and glanced across at Debbie, who was also grinning. He clapped his huge hands together and let out a roar of laughter. We started laughing, too. By the time he reached us, for no reason I could fathom other than he was laughing and we were following, we were in bits. You know the really unattractive laugh, the one where your face is wrenched into horrible spasms, your nose runs and your eyes water, and the only thing that's going to stop it is physical pain, so you start digging your nails into your palm and hitting your own leg? Well, that's where we were, and he hadn't even said anything yet.

It felt bizarre, but it felt really good.

When he calmed down enough to speak, he said in a broad Devon accent, "Yous made it here okay then?" which seemed like the funniest thing anyone had ever said and we were off again.

It took ages to calm down.

There's something wonderfully intimate about laughing with someone. He slung an arm around my shoulders and led me towards the pigs like an old friend. We even chatted as though we'd known one another for years, bypassing the "What do you do for a living?" formal style of questions in favour of, "Tell me, how're things?"

I told him we'd been living down here for eight months. I told him how different it was from living in London, and it was only when I'd finished the story that I realised that I'd told him about the dead chick.

"Happens," he nodded. "But it would've happened for a reason. Her wouldn't have been right. Don't beat yourself up, her would've died anyway, you just gave her an extra chance. I've never heard of anyone incubating an egg like that before. You did good. Unusual, ha-ha, but good!"

I smiled, and for the first time it felt okay to think about the chick. "We have lambs, too," I added.

"Tibbies?"

"Two of them," Debbie said. Then turning to me, "Tibby lambs are what they call orphan lambs."

"People dropped them off on the doorstep, can you believe that?" I said.

"Believe it?" he boomed, laughing deeply. "You bet I can believe it! What's your address, I'll be the next one round. Look, seriously, be careful or you'll end up with dozens of them. The price of lamb right now is rock bottom. Tibbies are worth nothing, and it's hard work and costly to rear them. It's simply not worth it. You two are a soft touch, just down from London and green as the fields — sorry, no offence meant. They know you'll look after them and you can afford it."

"What makes them think we can afford it?"

"Because you're from London," he said. With that he put a hand in the centre of my back and shoved me forwards. "There you go — pigs!"

I landed on the side of a make-do-and-mend pigpen. Part metal bars, part gates, part shower door (honest) and part wooden pallets all held together with strands of brightly coloured string, it was about the size of a garden patio. Inside, lying down with a bundle of baby piglets nuzzling and feeding from her, was the biggest pig in the universe. She was massive! Enormous! If you got four big men and squashed them together and remoulded them into the shape of a pig, you wouldn't be far out. She was about six or seven feet long and closer to 50 stone than 40.

I was speechless. I know I'm ignorant on farming and animals (I can't even remember going to a zoo as a kid, let alone a petting farm), but this big pig, lying there with her babies all bundled around her, was the most beautiful thing I had ever seen.

"You never seen a pig before?" he said.

I shook my head.

"Climb in. Go on, her'll be fine, hers used to all sorts."

I did as he said, careful to be as quiet as possible. Once in, I crouched down and stepped towards them. "What's her name?" I asked.

"Cynthia," he said.

I stopped and turned back. "Cynthia?"

"My wife named her."

"Okay, Cynthia."

At the sound of her name she looked up and grunted.

"Hello, pretty girl," I said, touching and stroking her head. I expected her to feel soft and pappy like the underarm of a fat woman, but she was solid. Behind me he climbed in, too.

"Here, let me hook one of the piglets for you." He scooped up one of the babies and shoved it into my hands. It wriggled and screeched as loud as the mandrake plant in Harry Potter. "Not like that, hold it tight to you," he shouted over the noise.

I wrapped my arms around it and cuddled it close. Straight away it went quiet and looked up at me.

"It's a little girl," he said, peering over.

A little girl with blue-grey eyes and long, thick, black eyelashes. I sat back cross-legged and cupped her to me like a baby. She felt warm, muscular and firm, and made me think of Tonka Toys from my youth, toys that were so well built they were said to be indestructible. She felt indestructible. She was so gorgeous I had this insane urge to squeeze her and sink my teeth into her bum.

"She's a little bruiser," I said.

"How many do you want?"

We spoke at the same time.

Debbie: "No, we're just —"

Me: "Two, I think —"

"Two's fine," he said. "Thirty-five pounds each. They'll be ready to leave mum in three weeks."

I looked up at Debbie, who was grinning and shaking her head, but in a way that meant yes.

"Can we have this one?"

"You can have whichever ones you want."

"How will I know which one she is?"

"Easy, hers half pink with black splodges on her bum. Take her and . . . how about that one over there, the one with a full black bum?"

Spotty Bum and Black Bum. Perfect.

CHAPTER
SIX

It was only when I got outside that I started feeling wobbly about what I'd done.

"I can't believe you did that," Debbie said in the car.

"Neither can I. Do you mind if we find somewhere to stop? I think I need a drink."

"You had such a go at me yesterday because you thought I'd got a lamb without discussing it with you first."

"I know. I don't know what's happening anymore. We never used to make decisions independent of one another. I don't know if I like it. I don't know if it's healthy."

"Well, you did it."

"I know."

We found a nice little place, ordered a couple of drinks and sat at a corner table.

"I should have let you hold her," I said. "You should have seen her eyes and her eyelashes and that little crinkled-up nose." I raised both hands and covered my face. "God, what have I done?"

"It's fine. Look, we were never going to walk out of there without having bought any, we both knew that."

"I didn't."

"You should have. I was taken aback that you jumped in so readily, but that's good. If you weren't keen, it would've been harder."

"I don't know that I am keen," I said, my hands still covering my face.

"But you loved them. I've never seen love at first sight happen before. It was beautiful."

"It was awful. I think I feel sick."

"Have a drink, you'll be fine. Now, I've done loads of research on the net into pigs and even found somewhere for us to go on a day's pig-keeping course and pencilled us in for next weekend. That gives you three weekends, less one day for the course, to build the house and get everything ready before we collect them."

Build a house. A house. Build. Me. Those words shouldn't be anywhere near the same sentence.

"Don't groan, you're not a child."

"I want my mum."

"Right at this moment, you'd probably be better off with a builder."

I did a face-wash motion with my hands and dropped them. "My life is out of control."

"Please don't be like that. Don't you feel like you're taking control? Don't you feel like you're doing things for yourself?"

I laughed so hard I choked. "No!"

"Oh, but you must," she insisted. "We're raising chickens for eggs and meat —"

"Meat? Who said anything about meat?"

"What do you think we're going to do if any of the chicks are boys? They won't lay eggs, and all they'll do is fight."

"All the same, I'm not sure I could eat them," I said.

"Don't be silly. Chickens for eggs and meat, lamb —"

"I could happily eat the lamb that nutted me . . ."

"And, in a few months' time, pork for sausages, ham, bacon, salami, that sort of thing. If that's not taking control of your life, I don't know what is."

Maybe she had a point, but I wasn't sure I wanted to see it. Neither did I want to argue. "Can we change the subject? I've just held Spotty Bum in my arms, and I don't want to talk about eating her already."

"But you know she's for food, don't you? You know that from the start, so it's not going to be a shock when the time comes — and don't name her, I forgot to say that. Apparently, if you name them, it's that much harder to send them off."

I sipped the drink. There were three or four customers around the bar who looked to be locals; other than that, the place was pretty much empty.

"Where's all this come from, Debbie?" I asked. "I can understand how you felt about work and the fact that you wanted out of London, but I never expected you to turn into a farmer. Since you've been down here, you've changed so much. Sometimes I'm not sure I know you anymore."

She reached over and took my hand. "Yes, you do."

I laughed. "I do?"

She did the little-girl-lost exaggerated nod, then said, "I didn't plan this. Despite what I said, I thought I'd have six months off and then find a position at a local solicitor's where I could carry on doing what I was before, only with a slightly smaller caseload and without the London stress. With you away so much, I spend a lot of my time on the Internet, and because I'm new to being down here, I go on countryside and downsizing forums. I've learned so much, and it's so exciting to be doing some of it, to get pigs and chickens and horses — *horses*! Remind me to tell you about horses!"

"What about them?"

She thought for a second. "I'll tell you later, it's not important right now. What is important is that I think this lifestyle will be good for us. It's much healthier and more natural. By producing our own meat, we're saving money, and the more money we save, the less time you need to spend away."

"I don't want to be a farmer," I said.

"I know you don't."

"I don't want to look like I'm a farmer either. I don't want to look like I live off the land or that I'm going back to nature."

"I know that, too."

The next time I was in London, I went to the hairdresser and asked them to shave my head all over. I also bought some smart black trousers, a pair of casual shoes and several crisp, fitted shirts. These, I decided, would be my weekend attire. No jeans, no sloppy trainers, no frilly purple shirts, no CND or Save our

Trees badges, no brown jumpers with patches over the elbows and *definitely* no long hair.

The pig-keeping course was fine. We learned about feeding and housing and looking after porkers. I even built the house. Me, I built it. Seriously! I got blisters and bruises, cuts and scrapes and cramp and everything. I pulled muscles, I got hot and sweaty, but still throughout all of it, I wore my smart new clothes. One has standards, you know.

One night after a long day of hammering nails, screwing screws, sawing wood, swearing, cursing and generally finding interesting and unusual ways to hurt myself with any tool I chose to pick up, Debbie remembered what she wanted to say about the horses.

I was lying flat out on the floor after an hour-long soak in the bath, thinking about all my aches and pains and wondering if there was a single limb that didn't feel abused.

"How was Georgie?" Debbie asked. I'd ridden her out first thing in the morning before going to work on the pig house.

"Fine. A bit strong, but we went for a good gallop and she calmed down after that."

"Would you like a horse of your own?"

"No."

"Think about it."

"I have. No thanks."

"Only we've been offered one. Georgie's mum actually. It would be a permanent loan, so no money need change hands. She sounds lovely. Everyone thinks she'd be perfect for you."

No, no, no. No way. "Not for me, thanks all the same. Who's everyone?"

"You know," she shrugged. "Don't you want to hear about her?"

"Not really."

"She's beautiful, and, um, she's just outside London . . . and I kind of said you'd go and have a look at her in the week."

"You're kidding? Debbie!"

"Don't whinge. Just go and have a look at her, please, for me?"

"I do these 'just go and look' things, and I always end up getting them. Look at what happened with the pigs. No, sorry and all that, but no. My safest bet is not to go and look at anything ever again."

Of course I ended up going. I finished work and drove the short distance out of London to see the horse. She was living alone in a stable beside this rambling old house. The stable was stone with a window at the back that had been removed so all that remained was the opening, through which the horse apparently spent most of her time with her head draped out, watching the world go by.

The first thing that struck me was how beautiful she looked. Light grey to the point of being white without a single blemish anywhere on her body, she had a long, silky, flowing mane, and these huge, deep, rich hazel eyes the size of saucers. And she was big. 17'3 hands big, which meant when I stood next to her, I couldn't see over her back. She was full Irish Draft, and her name was Roberta's Pride, but everyone called her Bobby.

I always hate this part of any transaction, the part where you're supposed to know the technical stuff. If it were a car, this is the bit where I'd be shown under the bonnet even though I haven't the foggiest what I'm supposed to be looking at, but at least you can blag that by wiggling a few leads poking out of the engine. But what was I supposed to do with a horse? She didn't have an engine. What could I wiggle?

Several horsey-type people had come out of the house and stood around the stable watching me. Even the horse looked expectant.

I walked around her nodding. Bobby, blimey, you're a big girl. I picked up her nearside front foot, spending several minutes inspecting the hoof. Then I did the same with the offside and pronounced them satisfactory. I rubbed her back leg, stroked her bum, ran my fingers through her tail, then made my way to her front, where I looked up her nose.

"Are you okay?"

"Oh yes, fine, thank you," I said, figuring I couldn't be that far out, there weren't that many things to look at.

"So what do you think?"

I stood back and took a long look at her. "She's wonderful. Truly beautiful," I said, and she was.

They all looked at one another, smiling. "Good. We've got your address in Devon. We'll send her along next week."

"What? Next week?"

"Can't get her to you any sooner, I'm afraid. Next week it'll have to be."

"Well . . ."

And that was it, I had a horse. Bobby arrived and settled in. Soon after, the pigs arrived, and while they didn't exactly turn up their noses at their house, neither did they go dashing into it — maybe they felt nervous that the draft caused by a dash might knock it down.

The ritual each Friday night when I got back from London was to kiss Debbie, cuddle my dog and then wander up and give a carrot to Bobby (and one to Georgie, she would have flipped if I'd missed her out), and a chocolate bar, or a cake, or something nice to Black Bum and Spotty Bum.

When the rental year was up on the cottage, we told the agent we wanted to renew for another 12 months. She seemed pleased (nothing cheers up an estate agent like easy money).

The pigs grew fast, and after five months they were ready to go.

After six months, they were borderline obese.

After eight months, we all knew if they didn't go soon, then the likelihood was they never would, which I would have been more than happy with. I loved them.

At some point, you have to make a decision.

You have to make a decision.

You have to.

One day, I loaded them into the trailer, and I watched it drive away.

CHAPTER
SEVEN

I know all the arguments, and I agree with each of them. Even the vegetarian ones.

If you're going to eat meat, then you should know where the meat comes from.

If you're going to eat meat, then it should be from happy, contented, free-range animals.

If you're going to eat meat, then you should give thanks and respect to that animal by enjoying every morsel.

If you're going to eat meat, then you shouldn't waste a scrap.

And, if you're going to eat meat, then you are a cruel, sadistic, barbarian only fit to roam the streets, knuckles grazing on the ground, with a club in your hand. Eating meat can be as simple or confusing as you like. I've plumped for confusing.

Watching the pigs go was the worst day of my life. I wanted to rush down the drive and stop the trailer, beg them to turn it around and bring them back. I didn't. Instead I shoved my hands into my pockets, turned and walked away.

I walked up to the stables — the opposite direction to the now-empty pigpen — and found Bobby eating hay. She nickered when she saw me, and I wrapped my arms around her neck and buried my face into her smooth skin.

I wanted to mourn and cry, wail and change into black, but it's difficult to do that on the one hand while the other is mixing a sauce that goes rather nicely with roast pork. It's strange how the mind works. Part of me felt sick at the thought of eating my friends, and the other part felt as though I had to eat everything so that it meant something, all the nice bits, but also the eyeballs, the anus, the ears and the trotters. Anything in between just felt wrong. It would be a week before the meat came back, which I decided was plenty of time to really screw myself up.

The following day I drove to London.

It was now 14 months since we had left London and moved to Exmoor, 14 months of commuting back and forth between work — London — and home — Exmoor. I was beginning to look forward to the drive between the different compartments of my life and felt comfortable in my car. In my car, I had CDs and sandwiches, sugary power drinks and the radio. It was neutral territory.

At work for the rest of the week after I had sent off the pigs, I ate vegetarian.

I knew something was up as soon as I arrived home on Friday afternoon and Debbie greeted me at the door with a quick kiss and three chocolate bars, none of which were for me.

"Come on," she said, taking my hand and leading me up to what should have been an empty pigpen. She was excited, which didn't bode well. "There," she announced, pointing, "is your very own pig. You can name her, you can love her, and we'll never get rid of her. We'll breed from her, and we'll have her forever."

Inside were three pigs, two pink ones and one black one. She was pointing to the black one.

"The other two are for fattening and keeping her company, but she's yours. What do you think?" she said. "Say something."

What I wanted to say was, *"What the hell did you go and do that for? I DON'T WANT IT!"* But I didn't. She was so pleased and so excited and thought she'd done something nice. So I thanked her, and she cupped her hands in front of her smiling face and bobbed up and down on the spot.

I smiled, too. What else could I do? I called the pig Kylie because she had a tiny, neat little bottom.

Chickens, Bobby and Georgie the horses, lambs, and now a Kylie pig. Life felt busy, and I found I'd started doing this mental diary tally thing at the beginning of each day:

Chickens: horrible and stinky

Bobby: gorgeous

Georgie: stroppy and constantly hormonal

Lambs: loud

Pink pigs: getting fat

Kylie: hates me!

Kylie hates me. I tried all morning, and she won't let me anywhere near her, and I can't work out why. She won't even take food from me. I feel bad, like it's my

59

fault and I'm letting Debbie down, so I try harder with her, and the harder I try, the more Kylie hates me.

How do you befriend a pig that doesn't want to know you?

I talked to her, I looked at her, I didn't talk to her, I didn't look at her. I smiled, I scowled, I lay down, I sat down, I stood up. I crawled into her bed and curled up, I even fussed the others in an attempt to make her jealous. Not a glimmer. It was only when I threw my hands in the air and said, "Fine. Suit yourself. I didn't want you anyway," and made to walk away that she even acknowledged I existed.

Having hung for a week at the abattoir, Black Bum and Spotty Bum were delivered back.

It was strange walking away from the new pigs straight into a kitchen where the portioned-up bodies of their predecessors were spread out across the work surfaces. There was meat everywhere, and not just any old meat but the fattest meat I had ever seen.

"It's white," I said.

"That's the fat."

"Blimey, is there any meat on it at all?"

Debbie held up a chop with a hand's width of fat running top to bottom.

"You could have a heart attack just looking at that," I said.

"The guy from the abattoir said for their age they should have come back around 70 kilos. One was 128, the other 136 kilos. I think we might have overfed them."

I didn't mind eating the anus and the eyeballs, but I didn't fancy eating all that fat. So was my only other option not to eat any of it at all? Somehow that didn't seem right either.

"However," Debbie continued, "We cooked a little and it is stunning! Try some."

She handed me a plate. On it was a trimmed chop cut it into bite-size chunks. The meat looked dark, much darker than any pork I'd seen before. It smelt gorgeous.

I knew everyone was looking at me, and I knew what they were thinking (which was the same thing I was thinking): could I do it? And the weird truth is, I wanted to. I wanted to eat it. More than that: I was excited about eating it. I scooped up a chunk and popped it into my mouth.

I felt energised, as simple as that. Maybe it's the hardwiring of the human man, the hunter-gatherer, the provider. I felt proud. I felt good and I felt strong. If these are bad things to feel, they didn't feel wrong.

Ignoring the fork on the side of the plate, I picked up another piece with my fingers and put it into my mouth, dribbling juices down my chin. Wow, it was good. I mean *really* good. It was creamy and succulent — and the flavour! To have anymore of a porky taste, you'd have to go out and lick a pig.

For all the months that this moment had been building up, I was convinced I was going to vomit on the floor the second I put any of it in my mouth, and now it had happened, I couldn't stop eating.

Don't get me wrong: I still missed my pigs. When I thought of them, my heart lurched and inside I crumpled. I felt sick at the thought that I'd not only sent them to their deaths, but I'd helped load them into the trailer that took them away. That day was still the worst day of my life, and I hated myself for it. Getting the meat back was different, like the two weren't connected; or they were connected, but there was much more of a distance than the actual week that separated them.

We packed the meat away, and that night, for the first time in a long time, there were no dreams of crashing planes.

Life settled into a pattern of commuting between London and Exmoor for the next couple of years, and I began to enjoy both parts of my life — until one day I was standing in the kitchen at home when the front door banged open and Debbie came darting in. Over time, I'd become less precious about my country attire, and while I still wore smart trousers and shirts in the evening, during the day I was more likely to be in riding breeches and a T-shirt.

I'd just got in from the stables and was fixing a sandwich.

"The land opposite is on the market," she blurted, slamming the door closed behind her. "We need to go and buy the local paper, that's where they're advertising it. We need to go now!" She yanked me in the direction of the door, then yanked me back and stood me still, gripping my arm until it hurt.

"The land opposite is on the market," she repeated, only louder, as though I'd just forgotten the language and, by shouting it, she'd made the statement clearer.

"I heard what you said."

"What do you think?"

It was a good question. It was the perfect location for us, so close I could look out of our bedroom window into the top field. Beyond that were some 10 acres of woods that ran down the steep side of the valley to the bottom where there were two further, good-size fields, a private road and a stream. Twenty acres in total. Perfect for us, perfect for pigs in the woods, and chickens, and fields for the sheep and horses. Perfect. But . . .

. . . But the money from the sale of our London flat was tied up in investments.

. . . But the tender was sealed bids, the most awful way ever invented to buy anything. Everyone interested in buying the land would write their full and final offer on a piece of paper and seal it in an envelope. On a particular day, at a particular time, all the envelopes are opened and the best offer is accepted. There's no second chance. From the position of the interested buyer, it's pure blind guesswork.

. . . But the land had been ignored for decades and was in a hell of a state without a strand of fencing on the place, or a gate that stood upright, which meant lots of work.

. . . But the guide price was high and was likely to take up every bit of money we had to buy it and put it straight. Still, we reasoned, when it comes to land, you can't really lose. After all, God isn't making any more.

63

We made a generous offer to secure it off the market prior to the sealed-bid auction and then sat stressing for three days while the owners considered it. Finally, they came back and said no, they wanted half as much again.

"You've got to be kidding!" I told the estate agent. "That's more than twice the guide price."

They didn't care. All they were interested in was the bottom line. If I wanted it, that was the price, take it or leave it. I told them in no uncertain terms that we'd leave it.

Putting down the phone, I said to Debbie, "That's it, we can't afford it. It would wipe us out. It would be crazy to go ahead."

If they had accepted our offer, I'm sure I would have felt uneasy and questioned the sanity of buying land in a county in which I didn't even want to live. But tell me I *can't* have it and I'll move heaven and earth.

We moved heaven and earth, and a day later I called back. "Okay, we'll take it."

CHAPTER
EIGHT

It took months to go through, and when it was finally completed Debbie and I walked the land together, holding hands and making plans. We worked out where the chickens would go. We imagined the horses in one field and the sheep in another. In the bottom section by the stream, we even found a whole other field buried under thorn bushes and undergrowth. That's how overgrown the place was. We had an idea we'd put the pigs in there and let them uncover it. It would probably take them a year.

"So who's going to do all the work?" Debbie asked.

Even to my townie eyes, it needed heaps of time, effort and money spending on it just to make it half sensible. It needed someone who knew what they were doing. It needed someone with skills.

"I'll do it," I said, thinking back to the house I built for Black Bum and Spotty Bum, and felt quite pleased with myself that I was prepared to take on the challenge considering I still didn't like being outside.

"You?"

"Yes, me. What's so funny about that?"

"Sweetheart, you've never even had a garden. I'm not sure you'd know where to start."

I kicked at a patch of long grass as though it were a football, missed, stubbed my toe on a rock and tried to pretend it didn't hurt.

"Come on, how hard can it be?" I said.

I hate looking useless, which, considering I'd spent the last 11 years working as an estate agent, was something you'd have thought I'd have got used to. Trying to hide my insecurities, I became indignant and refused to listen to offers of help. I think I even believed I really was going to do it all myself. I arranged four weeks off work and spent the Sunday before walking the land and working out what I was going to do. Even then I still felt confident.

Five minutes into Monday morning and I couldn't believe I'd been so stupid.

"You're back early," Debbie said as I kicked off my boots and flopped down on the sofa. I'd been gone half an hour in total. I felt useless — and I looked useless.

"You were right," I confessed. "I need help."

She took it that I needed help on the farm, which I wasn't sure was what I meant at all, but it would do.

Never one to shy away from a complete U-turn, I went all out to enlist as much help as I could lay my hands on. First, I phoned Ziggy, one of my brother's friends in London. Ziggy probably wasn't his real name, but it was the only name any of us knew him by. He was studying to become a lawyer, and he had a smart, college-boy look about him — at this point, the way people looked was still important to me. He was young, funny, confident and loved a drama. I mean *loved* a drama. His love life was so complicated even he had trouble keeping up with it, and every time it started sorting itself out, he added one or two more women to the mix to keep the tension high. I told him he needed a break. He didn't disagree.

I said I'd pay him well below minimum wage, but would make it up in bed, board and beer if he'd come down for the four weeks. He agreed and said he'd get the train tomorrow and be with us in time for dinner.

Next, we phoned around to see who was a good farming contractor. If you think country folk are a bit slow on the uptake, you'd be as surprised as I was when an hour later one of the contractors we had been given the number for, but had been unable to reach, turned up on the doorstep.

I opened the door, saw the huge belly with the grubby T-shirt that didn't quite meet the top of the jeans, heard the laugh and wanted to hug the man. Yes, it was the guy who'd sold us Black Bum and Spotty Bum, only this time he came bearing a name, Brian.

"I didn't know you were a contractor," I said, practically bouncing on the spot. Of course it was a stupid thing to say, there was no reason why I should know what he did to earn a crust. I'd just assumed he sold pigs.

Debbie made him tea, while I sat him down at the kitchen table and told him about the pigs and getting Kylie and the fact that she hated me.

"She doesn't hate you," Debbie called.

I whispered that she did hate me, and let's be honest, she did.

"What happened to your lambs?" Brain said.

"They went off, too. It's a shame as they were nice sheep. You know we ended up with eight in the end!"

He boomed with laughter and clapped his hand together. "Proper job!" he said.

"We got some more last year, they're in the field."

"Hoggets."

"Bless you," I said, thinking he'd sneezed.

Another boom of laughter. "No, hoggets. Year-old sheep are hoggets. Come along, Simon!"

"Are they?"

"You know they are," Debbie said.

I didn't. I'd never heard the term before in my life. Debbie put the tea in front of Brian and they began to chat. I was no longer part of it, how could I be, I didn't have a clue what they were talking about. None of it made any sense at all.

"Yes, well, of course the squiggly doo-dah and the oochy-coochy four hundred and ten were grug-bugglies." They carried on talking in this weird country code. It made me feel a bit thick.

There were terms for everything, and Debbie knew them all. She even used them in their correct place within the sentence, because he didn't laugh once. He just sat there, nodding, listening.

After half an hour without one word being directed at me, they both turned and asked, "Are you happy with that?"

Happy with what? I smiled. "Sounds good to me," I lied.

"Proper job!" Brian said, getting up and making to leave.

When he'd gone, I sat in gloomy silence, while Debbie buzzed about. I wondered what she thought of me. She must have known I'd never be able to do the work on the land myself. I couldn't even talk about it properly, let alone do it. I wondered how far ahead of me in all this country lark she was, and I wondered if I'd ever be able to catch up. I wondered if I even *wanted* to catch up.

"Why did you let me think I could do the work on the land?" I asked.

She stopped what she was doing and looked at me. "Because I know you could. I thought it might take a bit longer than the four weeks, but I figured if we did it together and worked as a team, we could do it."

The following morning I lay awake staring at the wall for ages before getting up. I decided I still liked Brian the Pig Man, who was now Brian the Contractor. It was impossible not to, and I'd put my trust in him and Debbie and roll with it. I had no idea where, when or how we would be rolling, but I'd go with it. Besides, I had an ally on his way, Ziggy!

All day I looked forward to dinnertime when he would be arriving. All through dinner I looked forward to him arriving.

"He's not coming, is he?" I said, getting into bed. "The git, he promised."

"Maybe the train was delayed or cancelled. Or he's ill."

"I hope it's nothing minor," I said.

Bang, bang, bang.

Bang, bang, bang.

It was two in the morning.

I got up, dressed and went downstairs.

"Did I get you up? Sorry, I know I'm late," Ziggy said when I opened the door, tossing in his rucksack and stumbling after it.

"You're drunk," I said.

He stood upright and wobbled. "Am I? Shit, I hate it when that happens. Can I have a drink?"

"Where have you been?"

"Ah, now that's a long story and definitely needs to be told over a drink. I met someone. Where's Debbie and the dog?"

"In bed."

"Shush then," he said, putting a finger over his lips and bundling past me into the kitchen where he spied some wine and helped himself. "I met this woman on the train. She was lovely, you know, classy, sophisticated. Join me for a drink?"

I shook my head.

"Anyway, while we were snogging she pinched my wallet and my phone. That or I lost them in the pub, which has never happened to me before. Are you sure you don't want one?"

"You were supposed to be here for dinner," I said.

"Good point. Is there any left? I'm starving."

I left him to it and crawled back into bed feeling like my ally might not be quite the good idea I'd hoped for.

Give him his due, in the morning he was bright and breezy.

"Good morning, happy campers," he sang, walking into the kitchen wearing jeans, a tweed jacket and a flat cap. He looked like an advert for a gun and country club.

"You look like a prat," I said.

"I look like a squire . . . No, you're right, I look like a prat. Seriously, what do you think? Borrowed from my dad. Thought they'd make me blend in."

"Like a local," I said, not at all sure what the locals would think when they saw him.

"So what's on the agenda?" he said, reaching for the coffee and slice of toast Debbie had made for him.

"First off, I want to show you around," I said.

I took him up to the stables and introduced him to Steph whom he kissed four times, twice on each cheek, hugging her and declaring, "I don't know why we don't do more things like the French. The British handshake is so boring."

"I'm glad you said that," I said, smiling at the glow in Steph's cheeks. "I want to introduce you to Kylie next."

He didn't kiss Kylie, but he did manage to stroke her, for which I hated him as I'd hardly been able to get near her since she arrived. I showed him Bobby, who wasn't taken in by him and made it clear she much preferred me, and Georgie who was indifferent to us both. Then I showed him the chickens and we collected eggs.

On the way back down the hill, I could see a commotion centred around the entrance to our land. There were trucks and a big digger, tractors and a knot of men standing around. We hurried down.

I recognised Brian in the middle of the group. When he saw me, he started waving, "Simon, Simon, over here."

I made my way to him.

"Us're going to increase the size of the gateway, wall up either side of it and put a proper gate on. Then we'll fence this top field, yes?"

"Okay," I said. "Did we know you were starting today?"

Removing his grubby baseball cap and scratching his head, he said, "Yes, yes, yes, yes," and nodded vigorously, which I took to mean no.

"You've done this kind of thing before then? This isn't the first gate you've ever made, is it?" Ziggy asked.

"Who's this?" Brian said, his trademark laugh deserting him for a moment.

"This is Ziggy. He's a friend who's come down from London to help. He's just kidding."

"I see."

With that, work began.

"Why'd you say that?" I said to Ziggy as we walked back towards the house.

"Come on, it was hardly a put-down, only a stupid joke. Didn't like it, though, did he? Methinks he doth protest too much!"

"He didn't protest at all."

"That's my point!"

CHAPTER
NINE

Back at the house Debbie made a tray of teas for the workers, after which Ziggy and I were set to work banging in fence posts at 10-pace intervals around the edge of the field, while the rest of the gang concentrated on the gateway.

After 1,000 years of hard-graft labour, Ziggy and I lay down on the grass for a rest.

"How many have we done?" Ziggy panted.

I looked up and counted. "Three," I said.

"Get up, Simon, no time for sleeping," Brian called at us.

"I bet he wears mirrored sun glasses," Ziggy said as we stumbled to our feet.

By the end of the following day the field was complete. Done. Finished. I think Ziggy and I banged in about six posts in total, but it was something.

I kept walking around it thinking, this is my field, *my field*. Something about the fact that it was fenced and gated changed the way it felt. I didn't even mind being outside, I didn't mind that I was dirty and sweaty and probably smelt, this was *my* field.

"You're not a horse," Ziggy called over the hedge. "Do you want a glass of wine or are you going to stick to grass?"

A few days went by while we waited for Brain and his gang to come back and start work on the bottom fields by the stream. To fill the time, we decided to prepare a celebratory dinner by cooking one of our own chickens. Which meant killing it first.

Ziggy and I walked up the hill to Steph's.

"What do you reckon is the longest stair lift ever installed? I'm sure they could fit one from your house up here," Ziggy said, puffing.

"We're looking at getting a quad bike."

"Cool!"

"Have you ever killed anything before?" I asked.

Ziggy blew his cheeks out. "No. You?"

I shook my head.

We walked the rest of the way in silence — if you don't count the wheezing and panting.

We still had the original batch bought when we first moved down, but they kept reproducing and we had more chickens than we could cope with. Specifically, there were four cockerels that needed to go because they were ragamuffins, fighting and squabbling all the time. Between us, we caught one of them. I held the cockerel in my arms.

"You wring its neck, right?" Ziggy said.

My heart was banging so hard I could feel it in my throat.

"I guess so. Should I stand it on the floor and do it?"

"Won't it run away?"

"Probably. Look, okay, right, I'll hold it, you do it."

"No way!" Ziggy said, showing me his palms and backing away.

"Well, I can't do it all!"

"Don't involve me, I'm strictly a KFC man: my chicken comes in a bucket surrounded by fries."

"I can't do it," I said. Then, "I've *got* to do it." I took a deep breath, put my hands around its neck and . . .

. . . and let go. I was right. I couldn't do it. The chicken looked at us and made a "parp-parp-parp" noise.

"You can't kill it now, it's just talked to you," Ziggy said. I let it go.

"Catch one of the others. I've got an idea," I told him and walked off. When I came back, I came back with an axe Steph used for chopping logs for the fire.

Ziggy caught a cockerel and together we held it down and I chopped its head clean off. As soon as the head came off, it started flapping like crazy in my arms. In the background I could hear screaming. Figuring it was me, I shut my mouth. The screaming, although half as loud as I was now silent, was still there. I looked up. It was Ziggy.

Then the weirdest thing happened. As soon as we looked at each other, we stopped screaming and started laughing. It wasn't funny — God knows it wasn't funny. I hated myself for killing the chicken. I felt sick. I think I wanted to cry. But I laughed. So did Ziggy. Not just laughter but hysterical laughter. We laughed until tears ran down our faces.

When we calmed down, Ziggy said, "That was the most horrible thing I have ever seen in my life."

"I feel bad for laughing," I said, for some reason feeling as though that was the worst thing I had done. "I don't know why I did. I'm so sorry."

"Adrenalin," Ziggy said. He was probably right, but I think I was more shocked at laughing than I was at the actual killing. What kind of animal was I that I could murder something and laugh, no matter how much adrenalin was involved? That's really bad. My hands were shaking so much I had to put the chicken down and walk away. I felt sober in a way that had nothing to do with alcohol.

How could I have laughed?

I went back, and we knelt with the chicken between us and began plucking its feathers. "Do you believe in God?" I said after a while.

"Dunno," Ziggy said. "Maybe, though if I'm known to Him at all, it's because the women I date all scream His name in bed, which probably isn't a great statement on my behalf. Everyone else catches His attention by praying. I catch it by screw —"

"Okay."

"Sorry. I'm just nervous. I've never done anything like this before. I guess, yeah, sometimes I do. Believe, that is. Look, surely it's okay to kill for food."

I shrugged. "I never used to believe in anything like that, but living out here, it's hard not to. There's so much life and death going on, you know what I mean?"

He nodded.

"Maybe one day I'm going to have to account for all this," I said. "Not the killing, I can get over that — I think — but the laughing."

"That's really messed you up, hasn't it?"

I didn't look up or answer. Yeah, that's really messed me up.

CHAPTER
TEN

We didn't eat the chicken that night, but we did the following night, and the weird thing was it was just the same as when Spotty Bum and Black Bum came back. There was a distance between what we'd done and the meal that was served up. It was gorgeous and we demolished every scrap. But I couldn't get the fact that I'd laughed out of my head. That night I woke from a nightmare drenched in sweat. I'd been in another plane crash, but this was the worst, most vivid, scary, real one yet.

The following morning we received a phone call from Brian the contractor. He was, he said, stuck on another job and was sending someone else over to start work on the bottom fields.

"I'll take Ziggy down and meet him," I said to Debbie. "While I'm gone, can you do me a favour — can you look into what we need to do to put Kylie in pig?"

Her eyebrows flew up.

"I need to, you know, do something good. Make life for a change."

She put her arms around my neck and kissed me. "I'm so sorry," she said. "I honestly didn't know it was going to be that bad for you killing the chicken. It was stupid of me to suggest it. I'll make sure you never have to kill another chicken, or anything else for that matter. I do love you."

I hadn't told her about the laughing.

"Keep an eye on Ziggy," she continued. "He's rubbing Brian and the guys up the wrong way — you don't think that's why Brian . . . no. 'Course not. Anyway, keep an eye on him."

"It's mutual. Brian and the guys are winding Ziggy up, too. There's a lot of sarcasm and one-upmanship going on. They think he believes he's better than them, and vice versa. They think he's a posh London lad, and he's playing up to it. If only they knew."

"As I said, keep an eye on him." I promised I would.

The man Brian sent had a big shiny new tractor and refused to take it anywhere on the land that might get it dirty, but he did have a post dropper attached to the back which meant we wouldn't have to bang fence or gate posts in by hand. Within three days, all the posts were in place. Then Brian came back to attach the wire stock fence to the posts.

Suddenly, the two fields down the bottom were done. We were a working, functioning smallholding — if an empty one.

"Us could clear that end mess of a field while we're here," Brian said. We were leaning against a post just far enough away from the others not to be involved in their conversation. Ziggy, whose voice had changed and was now ann-un-ci-a-ting b-e-a-u-tifully the Queen's English, was making up stories about his non-existent time at Eton.

". . . Prep was such a drag, and then one day Bentley refused to wear his tails, went to the Master and said . . ."

I started laughing.

"They can't stand him," Brian said. "Stuck up, thinks he's better than us just because he went to some posh school." Brian had become serious of late. I hadn't heard him laugh for ages.

"He's winding you up. He didn't go to Eton. He couldn't even tell you where Eton was, probably couldn't spell it either."

Brian nodded as if he'd suspected it all along. "He's still a prat."

I couldn't argue with that.

"This end field. Hell of a state. You want us to get it sorted?" he said.

"I think Debbie wanted to put pigs in there to clear it."

"Then that settles it. It's got to be fenced to keep them in. Us'll get the digger in presently. Proper job."

The digger came, and the digger dug. And dug. And ripped down trees, moved rocks and flattened the place. Flattened it all.

Debbie came down, saw what was going on and started crying. "What have you done?" she sobbed.

"I didn't do it," I said, bravely deflecting the blame. "It was Brian's idea. He said it needed fencing."

"Fencing yes, not destroying. That would have been free food for the pigs for months. Now we're going to have to buy in feed *and* pay Brian and his cronies for the work. We haven't got any money left. It's all gone. And I'm tired, so, so tired."

She grabbed hold of me, buried her face in my shoulder and let it all out while her fists pummelled my chest. I could see everyone watching, so I smiled over her back and put my thumb up.

To be honest, it was an awkward moment. But I cuddled her, soothed her and told her over and over again that it was all Brian's fault. Nasty man.

When she calmed down, she told me she'd spent the entire morning working out what we needed to do to get Kylie pregnant. No shock here: we needed a male. What *was* a shock was how easy it is to rent them on the Internet. Female pigs can rent a man. They even have photos of the boars with a brief description. Debbie had picked out a likely candidate.

Pedigree Berkshire boar. Muscular, kind and caring with GSOH. Can visit or accommodate. No time wasters please.

Okay, I added the GSOH, but other than that, it's pretty accurate.

The following day we loaded Kylie and took her to her Mr Right of Right Now. Kylie still didn't like me, and if I was honest, I didn't much care for her. Until I saw the boar. Suddenly I was terrified for her and was all for loading her back up again and taking her home. Debbie had picked her a real bit of rough — if he could have, he'd have been smothered in tattoos. Kylie, on the other hand, thought he was all right. She hopped out of the trailer, marched over to the boar and did everything bar lap-dance him. She wiggled her bum in his face, sniffed his bits and then screeched at the top of her voice in what I took to be, "Wow, big boy!"

I felt the need to apologise to the boar's owner.

"I'm so sorry, she's such a tart," I said.

He dismissed it with a shake of his head. "How old is her?"

"Fourteen months," I said.

"That's good. Perfect timing. He'll like she."

Evidently he did. Kylie shuffled about until she was comfortable, which was all the encouraging he needed before clambering on her back. I knew I should have walked away or at least turned my back. This was a personal, intimate moment between two — oh, sod it . . .

I watched, fascinated as his curly-whirly corkscrew penis came out, turning like a . . . you know those machines that dig oil wells? Well it reminded me of one of those. It kept going in, and kept going in, and *kept* going in.

I winced. I wanted to go in there, stroke her head and tell her it was okay and not to be frightened. But she didn't look frightened. In fact, she looked very happy.

We had two cups of coffee and an extensive tour of his set-up. We discussed payment and even sorted out leaving her for a while just to make sure she had fallen. An hour later, I nipped back to say goodbye to Kylie. They were still at it, still in the same position.

"I'm not criticising his technique or anything," Ziggy said behind me, "but personally I'd have —"

82

"Ziggy!" Debbie rebuked. Then she called out, "Be a good girl, Kylie. Mummy be back soon to pick you up." She didn't even notice we were leaving . . .

CHAPTER
ELEVEN

There is a reason why so few people own and work on a smallholding, and so many people live happily in city centres. Smallholdings are smelly, cold, rainy, isolated, lonely, dangerous and green, without pavements or streetlamps, or even electricity. I mean, how much further away from civilisation is it possible to get?

I was swimming against the tide of natural human evolution. I might have been doing something as inelegant as a doggy-paddle, but I was still going against the tide. While other people had iPads, iPods and iPhones, I had pigs, chickens and horses. When you're in a pub, boasting, it's difficult to impress with any one of those.

In London, I bought a chicken-and-mayo sandwich from a shop and couldn't eat it. I picked it up and made to put it into my mouth, but my hands wouldn't obey the command. Oh, I can chop off a chicken's head off, laugh, cook it and scoff it without too much trouble. I can fatten pet pigs until they're ready to be killed and eat them, no problem, but I can't eat a shop-bought chicken-and-mayo sandwich. Why not? Because the meat isn't home grown? Shouldn't it be the other way around: that I can't eat meat that I've been friends with and had a hand in killing?

I'm changing. I can feel that I'm changing. I just don't understand the way I'm changing. I don't understand the way I'm thinking. It doesn't make sense. I'm worried there might be something wrong with me. I wonder if I should see someone.

So I bought a dog. On impulse. And don't ask me *why*.

We went to a livestock auction to buy a ram to use with the sheep, and the last lot was a tiny, eight-week-old border collie puppy with only one eye. This big old farmer was walking around the parade ring with the dog in his arms, and everyone was laughing at him. Nobody wanted to bid for the dog.

"Because he's only got one eye, he's no good for working," Debbie whispered in my ear. "If he doesn't sell and they take him home, they'll shoot him."

The puppy was so scared he was shaking.

What the hell, I needed a friend; he needed a friend. I nodded a question at Debbie, who nodded back and smiled, then I put up my hand.

The auctioneer spotted me. "Hat thirty. Hat thirty. Hat thirty. Thirty-who? Thirty-who? Who? Thirty-who? Gentlemen, you surprise me, thirty pounds bid, do I see thirty-two? No?" *Bang* went the gavel. "Not sold."

I spun around to Debbie. "What happened?"

"You offered thirty, but it wasn't enough. They must have had a reserve on him."

"What happens now?"

"I don't know."

"Well, *I* do," I said, muscling my way through the crowd in search of the man. I found him outside still holding the dog. I offered him forty, he wanted twice that, we settled on fifty. I gave him the notes, and he handed me the bundle of black, white and tan fur, turned and walked away. No paperwork, no receipt, just thank you very much, here's a puppy.

I looked down into the puppy's little single eye and realised how lonely I'd been. Even Ziggy was picking up country things faster than me, which is why we'd left him in the middle field strimming stinging nettles, currently the only foliage I could positively identify on account of the, er, sting it gave you when you touched it.

But now I had a friend, and as it turned out, quite a fast friend. Border collies are sheep dogs, working animals used to running around for hours on end. And they're bright. Really bright. Our other dog, Darcy, is a Scooby-Doo dog, and will react with all the speed of a racing car off the line when you call, "Darcy! Cuddle-ups!" or "Puppy-sized kisses!" Ask him to sit, stay or fetch and he hasn't got a clue what you're saying.

I had a feeling this little chap would be different. First, I needed a name that suited him. I wanted something that meant fast, something nippy, but I wanted it to be a bit different, so I looked up the pharmaceutical name for speed, the street drug. There are a few, but the one that caught my eye was Dextroamphetamine. Dex! I'd call him Dex.

I asked my neighbour if I could keep Dex in the barn with their sheep dogs and took him up for the introductions. Everyone loves a puppy, and the three farm dogs that lived in the barn, Pip, Patch and Spike, were no exception. Then I introduced Dex to my other new baby.

Debbie knew how unhappy and confused I'd been feeling, mainly because I insisted on telling her every few minutes, so we had scraped some cash together and bought an essential bit of kit: a second-hand quad bike.

If you think that men never grow out of being children and are comforted with a new toy to play with, you're correct. Give a man a quad bike and no matter what else is troubling him, trust me, he's going to feel great. Strap a brand new, heavy-duty chainsaw on the back and he's going to feel even better.

"Excuse me, I'm just going to drive my manly quad bike around for a bit before I chop down a tree. Then I might kill something small and fluffy on the way home, I haven't decided yet."

The quad was a big, green, five-gear four-wheel drive and went like stink. We bought a trailer that hitched behind it, and suddenly I was mobile. The trailer was meant to carry tools and equipment about, and it did, but it also proved tempting for Ziggy, who insisted on travelling luxury class laid out on a straw bed in the back. The only dodgy moment came when I rolled the bike.

Quad bikes are ridiculously dangerous. Apart from the high-profile crashes involving the famous actor, or the even more famous singer, there have been many low-profile crashes involving not-at-all-famous farmers. None of the crashes are nice, though it tends to be only the farming incidents that end up fatal, and, like it or not, I was farming, so I was on the bad side of that particular statistic. Still, a boring stat like that shouldn't stop me from being a fool. And it didn't.

Two days after getting it and I was, though I say it myself, almost professional — professionally quick, that is. You just don't realise how many nip-about tasks need to be done throughout the day until you get a quad bike, and they all need to be attended to *as fast as possible*. With the trailer on, I drove like a granny. With it off, I drove like a speed freak who'd been told to hurry up.

The big no-no is to drive across the side of a steep hill. You only ever drive up, or down, because the centre of gravity is high up on the bike. If you go across the side of a hill, the bike just topples over. So you don't drive across a hill. Ever.

I drove across a hill. It might even have been okay if I'd been doing my usual Speedy Gonzales, but for some reason I was pootling — maybe on some level I recognised it was dangerous. As I drove, I felt the bike begin to tip over on one side, and it kept on tipping. They say accidents slow down everything; well, this one sped up. The more it leaned, the more gravity got a grip and the faster it began to roll over.

I tried to correct it, tried turning into the roll, but it was too late; if anything, the sudden change in steering made it tip even faster. So I did the cowards thing and abandoned ship. I just let go of everything and allowed myself to fall off. Funnily, you only feel scared afterwards. At the time, tumbling over the back while the bike underneath me carried on with its own forward and rolling momentum, I was more concerned that I'd trashed my new toy than I was for myself.

It was only as I sat up and watched the bike a few feet ahead of me succumb and roll all the way over, the handlebars digging into the soft ground and lurching to a halt upside down, that I thought, thank God I'm not underneath that.

Debbie was good about it, inasmuch as the injuries I sustained while telling her what happened weren't life threatening, though for a while I was concerned that my ear drums might perforate from the barrage of swearing and the amount of times she managed to fit the word "stupid" into each sentence.

"So you've had a bit of an adventure, have you?" they said on the phone — the garage came out the next day and fixed it. Then we were back in business.

"Drive slowly," Ziggy advised the following morning as we attached the trailer and filled it with tools and stuff. Ziggy dealt with the tools, I dealt with the stuff, which consisted of nice home-cured ham sandwiches, flasks of coffee, a four-pack of beer, a blanket, a bag of biscuits, a bag of cakes, a picnic blanket, a bottle of water, a first-aid kit with extra plasters, a tube of Germolene, the latest book by Nick Hornby that I was halfway through and, of course, my newest best friend, Dex. I have no idea what the tools that Ziggy dealt with were called, other than the fact that they were mostly made of metal and I owned them.

"Right, see you at lunchtime," I called to Debbie and, with a roar of the engine and a hoot of the horn, crawled away at about two miles an hour.

A minute later and we were back. Debbie hadn't even closed the door.

"What have you forgotten?" she said.

Ziggy got out and slouched past her, saying, "He's an idiot," loud enough for me to hear.

"Why?"

He threw out both arms. "Because he wants me to shave! What's he going to do, kiss me?"

She came out. "You're not going to kiss him, are you?"

"What? Of course not! I just don't want us to look scruffy, that's all."

"You're not in the office now, sweetheart," she said, touching my face. "Are you okay?"

"Yes. Probably."

"We'll talk later."

Ziggy returned, clean shaven, and climbed in the back without a word. We were off. Again.

Okay, so the tally stands at:

Two horses, Georgie and Bobby

One Kylie pig — currently away on a dirty weekend

Two fattening pigs

Chickens

Dex, my gorgeous, one-eyed puppy

Darcy, the mummy's boy great dane

Sheep

Maybe I'm getting used to it because it doesn't seem that bad anymore. I don't even feel depressed looking at it, which is kind of depressing. However, one thing is clear: now the land is all fenced and looking great, it's time to think about bringing our animals onto it. First, we need to create separate enclosures. I have no idea what happens if you put chickens in the same place as pigs, but I suspect you end up with fatter pigs and fewer chickens, which isn't ideal.

For the pigs I arranged to have a self-contained, movable pig house delivered, so all I had to do was build the enclosure around it. What could be simpler?

"This is going to be so simple," I assured Ziggy, who was looking at me with raised eyebrows as I rifled through the unfamiliar tools for anything that looked familiar. I picked up a hammer.

Together we paced out the perimeter. While Ziggy pushed plastic poles into the ground and banged them in with my hammer, I followed behind slotting bare wire into the keepers. When it was complete, I went around again, so we ended up with two strands of wire, one above the other, running through plastic poles that made up the perimeter of the enclosure.

Next we attached the wire to a pulsar and battery in a similar way to the chicken run I'd done all those years ago up at Steph's. (A pulsar is a clever electrical device that gathers up electricity from the battery and sends it out in single pulses rather than electrifying the fence with a constant current — which would empty the battery in less than a day and would hardly electrify the fence at all — kind of defeating the object.)

"Done," I announced.

"And that's going to keep in the pigs?"

"Of course!" I said, not at all sure that it would. Still, what's the worst that could happen? I was beginning to realise that that's such a stupid question to ask. It's like tempting fate with two fingers raised and your tongue out, especially when such a momentous moment had arrived — our own animals arriving on our own land.

Along with Debbie, we collected the fattening pigs from Steph's and made our way back down onto the land.

"The pigs are going to go nuts when they see this," I said as it did look wonderful. Within the electric fencing Ziggy and I had put up, the enclosure was massive and full of interesting bushes and trees, hollows and muddy areas in which to wallow. The house in the middle was big, light and airy, with a fresh straw bed all laid out nicely. This was porcine heaven.

Then again, maybe not.

I had thought that the worst that could happen was that the pigs would ignore the wire around the edge of their enclosure and wander off to destroy or eat something they shouldn't. Or that they would trash the place. Or kill their house. Or even kill each other. However, what actually happened was that they fell asleep on the journey down, so when I opened the back of the trailer with a fanfare, I found two snoring pigs.

Porcine heaven, it seemed, was the trailer.

I chivvied, cajoled and begged, and when it suited them, which was about an hour later, they yawned, got up, stretched and wandered out into their new world. They sniffed around for as long as it took to find their house and then went to bed.

"Oh." I said.

"I thought they'd go mad for it," Ziggy said, cracking open a beer to help restore him from the disappointment.

"So did I," Debbie added.

I was beginning to think that pigs were mighty lazy creatures. No wonder they ended up so fat.

Over the course of the next two days, everything came onto the land. Horses in the top field, sheep down the bottom in the middle field, chickens next to the pigs — we ran their electrified netting so there was a slim walkway between the pigs and the chickens. Ziggy kept getting zapped by the electrified wire and, on one momentous occasion, kept stepping backward and forward along the walkway between the two enclosures, getting zapped each time he hit the wire and yelping like a girly pinball.

Kylie came back from her Mr Right of Right Now the day before I was due to return to London after my four weeks away. I felt good about going back, like I needed some London work sanity.

Rather than sleeping on the journey, I found Kylie full of beans when I opened up the back. She bulldozed out and then set about bulldozing the other two pigs. She chose to inspect her new world by chasing the other two around it, biting their bums whenever she got close enough. Post sex, she was now a woman, and a woman who was not at all impressed that she'd been dragged away from her lover.

"Are you going to be okay?" I said to Debbie. We were in the bedroom, Debbie sitting on the bed watching me pack for London. "I'm leaving you with all the animals, and Kylie in a strop. It's all a bit unknown. The enclosures should be fine, but to be honest, if Ziggy and I built it, it only comes with a 24-hour guarantee, which runs out, um, about lunchtime. After that we can't be held responsible."

She smiled and looked up at me while I carefully folded five newly pressed white shirts. "I've missed you," she said.

"Don't you mean you're going to miss me?"

"No, I mean I've missed you."

I laughed, "Haven't we been together then?"

"That's not what I mean. It's been so hard with Ziggy living with us for four whole weeks. Love him to bits, but we haven't had any time together. And now you're going."

Five pairs of boxer shorts, five pairs of socks, packed.

"Haven't you missed me?" she asked.

"Um, of course, though it's kind of difficult to miss someone while you're with them."

"You're really looking forward to going back to London, aren't you?"

"No, of course not."

I was. I was insanely looking forward to London. The thought of a week of normality where I would hold conversations with people on topics other than pigs, chickens and stinging nettles was wonderful. I could dress like a human being in a sharp suit, wear shoes instead of welly boots, sit in a warm, dry office and hold a pen — oh, how I missed holding a pen!

94

"You are looking forward to going. I can tell. I know you are."

"Look, I'm not, really I'm not." I wonder why there's so much comfort in such a simple act as holding a pen? Something to do with being ready, being prepared, being in control? All the things I missed.

I was to drop Ziggy off in London on the way through, so the three of us made a final tour of the land. We patted and stroked and said goodbye to all the animals. My mood with the thought of going back to London was soaring high.

"You will miss me, won't you?" Debbie said as we hugged and kissed next to the car.

"Millions," I said, and that part I really meant.

I dropped Ziggy off in London, and he promised that any holidays he had from college, he would spend down with us helping out. I agreed, though I wasn't sure what Debbie would say. Then he floored me by saying that he loved every second of being on Exmoor. "You're a complete prat for not realising how lucky you are." He said and slammed the car door shut.

There wasn't much I could say to that other than poke my head out the window and call him an idiot, which I did. Then I sped off.

CHAPTER
TWELVE

A four-week absence in any office is a long time, but in estate agency it's a lifetime. Everything had changed. All the buyers I'd known had bought their properties or had started looking elsewhere. All the sellers had sold. There were new houses on the market I didn't recognise, and new sales progressing in the cabinet I knew nothing about. It was horrible.

Despite that, it felt good to be in London and it felt good to dress smartly, but it kind of ended there. Maybe the thought of it was better than actually being there. I kept thinking of home, kept finding reasons to nip out so I could call Debbie and get updates.

I missed Dex (God, how I missed my puppy). And Bobby, even Kylie, even . . . okay, the chickens are a miss too far. But only just. I was that far down I even missed Ziggy, which isn't easy.

I missed Debbie the most. I missed talking and planning what we should be doing each day. I missed laughing — people at work in London just don't laugh, at least the people in my office didn't. I missed the fear of each day, the fear that an animal would do something important and I would miss it. Somehow not spotting something that one of them was trying to tell me, to communicate to me, seemed unforgivable.

Lets face it, anyone can react to a problem and call in a vet, but spotting a problem early enough to solve it before it happens by reading a situation and listening to what the animal is trying to tell you, that's what makes a difference. It's that terror of missing something that I felt, even if I didn't realise that's how I felt until right there and then.

How come everything seems so clear when I'm sitting in an office in London and I couldn't figure it out when I'm there, at home?

I missed the air of Exmoor (office air conditioning is so stuffy). A small part of me even missed being outside. I felt unsettled in London. I felt out of place. I felt . . . I felt like I didn't belong there. But in the same breath I *did* belong there. London is my home. It is my world. The streets and the people are what I understand. The whole situation was confusing.

In a moment of unbelievable weakness, I agreed with Debbie that we should get more chickens. And some ducks, some geese and some turkeys. Debbie ordered them, and a week later we drove around and collected masses of poultry, to the point that we renamed the front field the "chicken field".

They were everywhere: ducks whack-whacking, geese honking, dozens of chickens cock-a-doodle-do-ing, and turkeys eating, which is about the only noise turkeys make, other than their gobbly chatting sound, but they don't tend to do that with their mouths full, so it doesn't happen often. On top of that, my dog Dex would run around barking. It was loud. The field is about the size of a football pitch, so there was plenty of room, but even so, when they were all at it, it sounded like a naff orchestra tuning up. You could hardly hear yourself think.

We bought a stunning cockerel that had so many different licks of flaming red feathers over him he almost seemed as though he was on fire. We called him Red. His job was to look after the hens, and boy, did he take his job seriously. He was a shag machine. From any perspective, his dedication to love every female at least three times a day was eye-wateringly impressive. This was not a boy who wanted a cup of tea and a chat. One time, I watched him do the deed with one female and then hop from her back onto the back of another and start on her without even touching the floor. If there were such a thing as a sex Olympics, this cockerel would be a gold medallist.

"We need more pigs," Debbie said, while we were letting out the animals one morning.

"That's nine in 10 minutes," I said, keeping one eye on the stopwatch mode on my phone and one on Red, who leapt off one hen and ran across to another.

"Will you please stop counting the number of times he makes love?"

"That", I pointed out, "is not making love. The boy's a phenomenon. I'm his manager. I'm thinking of putting him in for a competition."

"Don't be silly. It's natural. It's what they do — actually, it's *all* they do," Debbie said.

"Get out of here! It's not all he does," I said, feeling very protective over my boy.

"Well, have you seen him do anything else?"

"Don't be like that."

"I'm not being like anything. Really, it's all that males do," she insisted. "Now, can we talk about getting more pigs?"

"Not while you're being spiteful."

"How am I being spiteful?"

"By saying males don't do anything other than sex. It's such a stupid cliché."

"What else has he done?" she said.

"It's just he hasn't got time for anything else right now. He's probably got really big plans for when he retires."

"When he retires?" she shrieked. "Look, we need one cockerel for all these hens. The girls are important, they lay the eggs. His job is to be sexy with them, and I grant you he is dedicated. But that's all he's good for."

"So he's a sex object? Use him and abuse him?"

"They're hardly begging him to hang around after, are they? He's very pretty, but he's a bit thick."

I looked over just as he moved across to another lady.

"Maybe in the chicken world that's true, but it's not the case for all males, you know?"

"It pretty much is in nature — and we are talking about nature here. You're not going all insecure and comparing yourself to a chicken, are you?"

I huffed, not prepared to dignify that with an answer.

"Oh, sweetheart . . . Look, all I want to talk about is getting more pigs and putting them in the woods."

"We've got enough pigs. We don't need anymore, and we certainly don't want them in the woods," I said and slouched off.

We got pigs and turned them into the woods. Two new sows with piglets at hoof. It was perfect timing because Kylie was getting bigger and was at the point in her pregnancy of needing to be on her own, and her two companions were ready to go off.

It's quiet when pigs leave. Eerily quiet. This time, however, I knew it would be easier because I had remained distant. I was crazy getting so close to Black Bum and Spotty Bum. Madness. This time it would be fine.

I loaded them, took them to the abattoir myself and cried so hard on the way home that I had to pull over because I couldn't see. I sobbed, and sobbed, and sobbed. I hated it, and I hated myself for doing it. All the same feelings I had with Black Bum and Spotty Bum came rushing back. Why, when I'd so carefully not made friends with them? I thought again that this smallholding world was too raw for me. I wasn't born to it — is it even easier if you are born to it? I didn't know, but I guessed it must be or everyone would be vegetarian.

I drove straight back down onto the land and crawled into the house with Kylie, who — unused to the extra space in bed without the other two — was stretched out, sleeping in the straw. She knew I was there, but didn't try to pull away or even move. I sat cross-legged beside her and talked and told her everything I was feeling, even the really confusing bits. It was a long afternoon. I don't know if I understood any of it any clearer, but I did feel better afterwards. I kissed Kylie's cheek, thanked her for listening and crawled out. It was only afterwards that I realised that was the first time she had ever let me touch her.

"Let me get this right," I said some time later, still unable to comprehend the roles of males and females in nature. "Men are just nooky, while women do all the worthwhile things like giving birth and rearing children."

Debbie thought for a second, a very short second. "That's about it, yep."

"Aaahhhh-ha! What about the big cats in Africa? What about when they catch a gazelle for dinner!"

"No, that's the females, too."

"Is it? Are you sure?"

"The females do all the hunting. Does it upset you that women use men for sex, and that's all men are good for?"

"In nature," I add.

"If you like."

"Debbie!"

She was never like this when she was a solicitor.

I feel like I'm changing, too. I kind of hope I am, though it's difficult to monitor when you're with yourself all the time. It's like watching your own child growing up and getting taller. You don't notice the small, daily increments until suddenly you look and think, they're nearly as tall as me, when did that happen?

I could spot the big changes in myself easily enough: for instance, before we moved to Exmoor, I thought the most naturally beautiful woman in the world was Catherine Zeta-Jones. I still think she's the most beautiful woman in the world, but if you asked me what the most beautiful *creature* was, it would be my horse Bobby.

I've never thought of an animal as beautiful before. Certainly not a specific animal. But when I look at Bobby, it's like looking at an incredible piece of art; a painting or maybe a sculpture, something that takes your breath away no matter how many times you look at it. When I look at Bobby, my heart melts.

Debbie was still working at Steph's, cooking for the guests, so it was easier to stable the horses up there when the weather was bad. The guests were predominantly women who wore skin-tight riding trousers that showed off their gorgeous bodies (horsey girls are wonderfully sexy, you know).

Anyway, I was up at the stables one day, Debbie was cooking, and I was brushing Bobby, when I had an idea. I thought, I'll ride her bareback without a saddle. I tacked her up with bridle and reins, nothing else. Then I hopped on her back, no hat, just breeches, knee-length leather riding boots and a white shirt untucked. I felt really close, like I was part of the horse. She, in turn, felt looser, freer without the saddle as a barrier between us.

I took her outside where a large group of thirty-something women were standing around, waiting to be assigned their own horses for a ride. I paraded

Bobby past — actually, I paraded Bobby through them. We looked fantastic. Dashing. Incredible. In fact, I decided we looked so dashing and incredible that I turned Bobby around and walked back through the girls for a second time.

Honestly, I could have held out my hand and picked any one of the women and lifted them up behind me and they would have gone with it in a heartbeat. I was Richard Gere in the end scene of *An Officer and a Gentleman* mixed with Colin Firth when he climbs out of the lake in *Pride and Prejudice*, all on horseback. I was magnificent. I was every woman's sexual fantasy. Bobby suddenly dropped a shoulder, and I was ... falling ... and ... sitting in a puddle, with Bobby looking down at me, snorting.

I was soaked. My skin-tight and sexy breeches went all baggy around the bum, so it looked like I'd filled a nappy. My shirt was plastered. My boots were grey and drenched, and ooze had trickled down inside, squelching when I walked.

Utterly humiliated, I padded back through the group of hysterical women, leaving a muddy trail of footprints in my wake, leading Bobby. The girls were laughing so hard they were either crying or about to wet themselves.

I led Bobby into her stable and untacked her. I didn't talk to her for three days, just did everything around her in silence. Then, on the fourth day, I turned to her and said, "You utter, utter bitch!"

She tossed her head in the air and snorted.

"It's not funny."

She did it again.

"For the first time in this miserable, stinking, country-bumpkin world, I felt good. I felt great, and you go and make a fool of me."

She put her head down so her chin was on the floor and waggled her whole head and neck, her mane flicking back and forth.

I leant against the wall, slid down so I was sitting level with her head and smiled. "I guess I did look a bit of a prat," I said.

She raised her head and did the tossing, snorting thing again. Then she moved and gently nudged me with her nose. I got up and groomed her, brushing and pulling her hair until she fell asleep where she stood.

That night, Debbie complained she couldn't sleep, so I did the same thing, running my fingers through her hair and stroking her back until she nodded off. Females are really quite similar, I have noticed.

The only females I knew who didn't like to be stroked to sleep were the hens, and only then because they were kept too busy by Red.

I could watch the chickens for hours. They were so funny, and Red was just a sex machine. I thought the hens would tire of him, but not a bit of it. They almost lined up for him. First thing in the morning I'd drive down onto the land and let all the chickens out of their houses. It is a nice way to start the day. When I first got Dex, I'd drive the quad bike with him perched in a basket on the front, but it wasn't long before he decided to take matters into his own paws and started standing on the seat behind me while I drove. Maybe he felt that if I crashed, he wouldn't be the first one to hit the wall. Sensible lad.

Early one morning, I drove down and parked up at the gate as usual. Dex jumped off the back. I could see shapes all over the grass. I unlatched the gate and walked in. The shapes were chickens. They were all out, and all asleep all over the ground. How odd.

I walked up to one. Her head was missing. Her chest was ripped open, and all her insides had been eaten. What I had mistaken for sleep was death. I didn't know what to do. Dazed, I started walking between the bodies, not doing anything when I reached them other than stand over them and look down. Then I moved on to the next one.

I walked to the chicken house. The wire that surrounded it had been ripped back to create a huge hole. There were more dead chickens inside. Blood was splattered everywhere. I found Red just outside, his flaming red and orange feathers rolled and caked in mud and blood, his body half eaten.

"Oh God, not you, Red, please, not you," I whispered.

Every single chicken was dead. Every single one.

CHAPTER
THIRTEEN

I tied Dex up and went to get Debbie. She cried, and I felt as though I'd lost all sensation, like it had been switched off. You could have put out a cigarette on my arm and I wouldn't have felt it. The only physical feelings I had were on the inside, where I felt shivery cold. But if my physical feelings had been shut off, my emotions had been cranked up to maximum, and they were burning hot.

A fox had got in and murdered them all. I wanted to kill the fox. With raw anger, I wanted to slam its head onto the ground and *stamp it into the mud*!

They were just chickens, for Christ's sake. Defenceless chickens. They were so happy. How could they all be dead?

I picked up each one and carefully laid them in a pile. There were 36 bodies in total. I recognised them all: Doris, whose chick Debbie hatched between her boobs; the one with the droopy wing; the one that wouldn't get out of the way when I walked around the chicken field; the one with the sore back who was either Red's favourite or too slow to run away; and, of course, Red himself.

The field was so quiet without them, and so empty. I sat next to the pile feeling horrible and angry, sad and empty all at the same time. It was the worst I'd ever felt.

I spent ages cleaning and strengthening the chicken houses until I'd have struggled to break in myself, let alone a fox. Chickens are stupid things. But life without them was a duller, less funny place. As soon as we could, we'd get some more. The rest of the poultry — the ducks, turkeys and geese were all kept separately, so at least they were safe. For weeks afterwards, they were subdued, not venturing far away from home.

Ducks, as birds, are really rubbish. They flap their wings, but, even on a good day, are unlikely to get more than a hand's breadth off the ground. They also stick close together in a group; they are really very good friends and just waddle about in a gang all day. Which, I realised, made them perfect to teach Dex some rounding-up skills before he was big enough to work the sheep. Great plan!

Every night for a week I tied Dex to my belt so that he had to run where I went, and I'd shout the commands in real time as I rounded up the ducks and drove them into their house. The commands were: left, right, forward, stop, stay, steady and away. Simple.

When the week was up, I decided Dex was ready to fly solo.

The ducks were over the other side of the field. I held him by his collar, threw a pointed finger out in front of us and commanded, "Dex, *away!*"

107

He ran away . . . to the duck house where he lay down in the doorway, chin on paws. Nice, get a sheep dog and do the work yourself. I trudged off to the far side of the field to find the ducks. I found them soon enough as they are white and hardly camouflaged to the environment. I made my way behind them, put out both hands, ready to start herding them towards the house, and stopped. I could see Dex watching me. Maybe . . .

"Forward!" I shouted and moved forward, confident Dex would be watching and learning.

The ducks bolted to the left.

"Left!" I yelled, running left. "That's it, boy, good boy, keep running left." I kept running left and caught up with the ducks again.

"Stop! Stay!" I stopped and stayed, standing still and glancing up at Dex to make sure he was still watching me. He was.

"Okay, good boy! Forward . . . steady . . ." I moved forward, steadily. Suddenly, the ducks bolted right.

"Right!" I ran right, caught them again.

"Steady!" I steadied.

"Now, forward, slowly." I moved a bit too quickly and the ducks tripped over themselves trying to run. "I said *slowly*!" I yelled, slowing down. "Good. Good boy!"

Bit by bit I manoeuvred the ducks down to the house. When I got there, I discovered that Dex had got bored and nodded off. I had to shout to wake him up before the ducks would go in to bed.

Forget the roles of males and females: I couldn't even establish those of man and dog.

Man and his pig, however, is a different matter as three months, three weeks and three days after Kylie met her boar, she gave birth.

It was terrifying and gruesome, mucky and wonderful all at the same time. Frankly, an egg hatching between Debbie's boobs was no preparation for this.

When Kylie didn't come out to eat and just lay in her house, groaning and with milk leaking from her teats, it was obvious even to me that she was imminent. I sterilised my hands, crawled in with her, knelt down at the business end and waited.

They really strain when the contractions come. I kept nipping up to the head end to stroke her brow and tell her she was doing brilliantly — I had no idea if she was or not, but you can hardly admit to a woman in labour for the first time that you've no idea what you're doing. Hardly say, "I once saw a lady give birth in an episode of *ER*, so it should be okay," even if they are a pig.

Then, out of nowhere, a piglet shot out the back. Well, not out of nowhere, obviously, but I mean there was no warning. I think I'd expected a countdown, but you get nothing, just, bang! There's none of this "I can see the head" malarkey. It just opens up and a piglet fires out and lands about a foot behind. Seriously, you could kneel back there like a wicket keeper and catch them. The piglet was still in its sack, a milky white membrane that it needed to get out of in order to breathe and start life, but it was shattered. The trip out must be hard work.

I gently teased away the sack until the pig's little face was clear, and it slithered around to the milky teats, stuck its mouth on one and began feeding. Who could blame it? It had been in there growing for a smidgen under four months so it must be nice to get a solid meal inside it.

Kylie shot out four more, then rolled over and shot out another four. Then came the afterbirth, which is disgusting. I'd heard that some mothers eat their own afterbirth. Having seen Kylie's, I wouldn't recommend it.

I sprayed nine little navels with an antiseptic spray, and when they were all happy and fed, and formed themselves into a clump over to one side, asleep all higgledy-piggledy on top of one another, Kylie got up, sniffed her babies and came over to me snorting manically, telling me what she'd done.

"I know, I know. You're so clever," I said, ruffling her forehead and pulling her ears. "You're so clever." She snorted in my face and I carried on telling her how brilliant she was. Then she turned and went back to lie down again.

Sitting in the straw with the fresh clean smell of birth in the air, I felt the same as you feel when you've read an intimate book about someone's whole life, and you've read it in one sitting. I felt bigger, like I'd expanded somehow. It's a profound and moving experience for a city boy like me to play midwife to an animal. There are people in London who wouldn't even

110

trust me as an estate agent to negotiate the price of their curtains, yet here was an animal who was prepared to let me help her with her most precious things in the entire world, her babies.

It made me feel confident, and I carried that feeling around with me for days after. I felt warm on the inside, which, after the attack on the chickens, was nice. It was also handy as on the outside I was freezing and soggy because it hadn't stopped raining for weeks. It rained so hard that, one night, when I was walking along the path in the direction of the pigs with a bucket full of feed at my side, I didn't even see the big black sow trotting towards me until it was too late.

One second I was walking and upright, the next I was bulldozed over and sitting in a muddy puddle, the sow at my side scoffing feed from the bucket in huge, gulping mouthfuls.

"What is it with these animals that make me sit in stupid puddles!" I yelled. "Get your nose out of there! How did you get out, anyway?"

I scrambled to my feet and yanked the bucket away before she had the chance to eat the lot. Then, walking with that stiff-legged, slightly open gait typical of moving about with wet underwear on, I made my way, sow at my side, to the pig enclosure.

I immediately saw what had happened. A branch of a tree had come down right across the electric wire around the perimeter and shorted out the system, rendering it useless and thus allowing the pigs to wander off. I tossed the food in the trough where all the pigs dived in to eat and walked over to the branch.

I had to move the branch to get the electric fencing working again, but it was big and awkward and wet. I tried yanking it and pushing it without any joy — it was just too heavy. So I stood over it, legs either side of the wire, and tried lifting the branch that way.

As the branch came up making the electric fence live again, I sank down on my haunches like a weightlifter. The wire came up, I went down. The wire came up, my soaking wet bum went down. More than that, the wire came up, my soaking wet bum and soaking wet underwear containing soaking wet male delicacies that have no business going anywhere near an electric current (especially when wet) went down.

Live electric current and soaking wet testicles connected in a shower of sparks (I might have imagined that bit) and a scream that was so high pitched dogs several miles away looked up to the sky and howled (I didn't imagine that bit).

"Aaawwoollllllllllll!"

CHAPTER
FOURTEEN

"I could have been killed," I tell Debbie, exaggerating as only a man can when his bits have been jolted by a mild electric current. I'd changed my wet jeans to loose trousers and perched myself on the edge of the sofa, legs wide apart. "It's not funny."

She doesn't agree. There are tears of laughter running down her cheeks and she's flapping her hands in front of her face. But at least she's calmed down enough to speak. "My stomach hurts, I've laughed too much," she complained.

"Good."

"Oh, sweetheart. Go on, tell me once more, you really straddled an electric wire and sat on it?" and she was off again.

"Why's it so funny?" She doesn't answer. I'm not sure she can.

I look down. "The sperm will all be dead. Electrocuted. It's how they kill prisoners on death row, you know. Only the prisoners get a chair, my sperm didn't even get that."

"They're not necessarily dead. They treat depression with electric shock therapy. Maybe your sperm will just be a whole lot happier." She lost it again, this time rolling around on the sofa howling with laugher, holding her sides and spluttering, "Smiling sperm . . . telling jokes to each other . . . party hats . . ."

I'm due back in London tomorrow, but I'm not sure I should drive. If I don't go, what am I going to say to them in the office? I can hardly tell them the truth, "I'm afraid I'm going to be a day late. I seem to have electrocuted my testicles."

Besides, I needed London right now. I needed the fix.

In London, when you have a bad day, you have a bad day. That's it. Here, you have a bad day and something dies, or you kill it, or you send it to be killed, or you nearly kill yourself. In London, I hardly ever nearly killed myself. Or anything else for that matter.

I did a quick tally:

Two horses, Georgie and Bobby

One Kylie pig with eight beautiful babies

Two sows with piglets in the woods

Dex, my gorgeous, one-eyed puppy

Darcy

Sheep

Ducks

Turkeys

Geese

Chickens — none

I miss the chickens. I've calmed down a lot, and I'm more rational about it all now. I'm still angry, but I'm also embarrassed about the whole "stamping the fox's head into the mud" thing. I think I want to get some more chickens.

The rest of the animals, I'm getting on okay with. Some of them better than okay.

Since giving birth, Kylie has become my best friend. I spent ages on Google the other night and found out pigs have seven sounds with which they communicate, although they mostly express themselves through body language. I'm trying to learn both.

I've never heard a pig oink. Never. If anything, it's more a woof, or a screech, or even a bark, but never an oink. Where did the oink come from?

There's a noise they make when they first see me and I don't know if it means, "Hello!" or "Here comes a bucket full of dinner!" It's a scratchy, whiney, oof-oof-oof. Their body language is excitement, running around, so I guess it's food related and not me. They do love food.

I watch what the pigs do and say to one another in the woods, and then I go back and copy it to Kylie. Sometimes she gets it, and sometimes she's confused. I don't blame her, I'm a terrible mimic.

Walking into her enclosure, I bend forward like an old person on a bowling green executing a long follow-through, pigeon-step forward and make the oof-oof-oof noise. I do it quietly — to someone who's never heard English before, the phrase "Hey, everything's okay, I just want to be your friend" probably sounds similar to "You want me to cut your head off or what?", so I figure it pays to be careful.

Most of the time Kylie just looks confused.

The one noise I *have* got sussed is a swearword — isn't it always the first thing anyone learns in a new

115

language? It's a short, sharp squeal and roughly translates to "Sod off!" Pigs do it among themselves all the time, and when one of them tries to eat my boot or trip me up, I do it to them. The first time I did it all the pigs came and gathered around me, then started barking and woofing. I wasn't sure if they were mocking me or joining in. Now when I do it they tell me to sod off back. It's very amicable.

Yet not being able to mimic anything above a swearword with any level of competence is a bit of a problem. What about the other part of animal communication, the body language? Surely I could learn that?

Here's the deal, I know I'm never going to be fluent but what I'd like to be able to do is stop the pigs from dive-bombing me whenever I go into their enclosure without telling them to sod off. I know I'm only copying what they say among themselves, but there's got to be a better way.

I watched the pigs for hours, but couldn't figure it out. When one pig was approached by another pig and didn't want to be bothered, it went aggressive, making chomping motions with its mouth and physically driving the other one away. I tried the same. All that happened was that they got more aggressive back, something that rarely happened when the pigs did it among themselves. In a fight against a 40-stone sow and her bruiser sons, I was always going to come off second best, so I stopped trying to copy that.

In the end, I did go back to London the day after my testicular electrocution. I took lots of painkillers. Even though I wasn't in pain, I felt as though I should be and figured it's better to be safer than sorry — and wore thin, comfortable trousers. During the whole journey I thought about how I could communicate to the pigs that I wanted some space when I went in with them, without resorting to swearing or aggression.

As it happened, I found the answer in a London pub.

After work one night, I'd decided to stop off for a bite to eat and a beer in a nice trendy bar. The beer was easy to choose; the bite to eat was more complicated. I was still having big problems with food and couldn't eat meat away from home, even though for all of my life meat had been my staple and I don't want to be a vegetarian. I think I understand it a little more now and know that it has something to do with animal welfare. I also know that it has something to do with the processes some commercial meat goes through, and I know it has something to do with feeling uncomfortable at the thought of all the additives. What I don't know is in what percentage each part troubles me.

I ordered the vegetarian pasta and sat back to wait.

At the bar, two scenarios were playing themselves out. In one, a couple of guys were squaring up to each other, while at the other end of the bar, a guy was chatting up a girl.

The men squaring for a fight were standing toe to toe, shoulders back, faces pushed forward, fists clenched by their sides.

In contrast, the guy chatting up the girl had rounded shoulders, head pointing slightly down, standing side on to the girl, and he was smiling. She was sitting on a stool not facing him, but with her knees pointing in his direction. She was also smiling.

You didn't need to hear the dialogue to know the men were aggressive and the couple passive.

I clearly recognised some of the square-set features of the aggressive men in myself when I went into the pigs' enclosure. I guess in a way I was scared of the pigs: they're massively strong animals, so I think I was trying to cover that up and show them who's boss by making myself look confident. Only I could see it didn't look confident at all: the guy who was by now doing rather well with the girl didn't seem lacking in confidence just because he looked passive; if anything, he looked more confident than the idiots about to knock each other's blocks off. Equally, my body language with the pigs wasn't confident, I could see now that it was aggressive.

No wonder the pigs were bolshie when I went in with them, they were reacting to my aggressive lead.

The more I thought about it, the more convinced I became that I was right, and the more excited I became that I'd cracked it. I couldn't wait to get home and try it out. I still had days to go at work, but the good thing was that when I did go home, I would be back for three weeks as it was coming up to Christmas, the quietest period for an estate agent, and I'd sneaked off a couple of extra weeks.

"I want to do you a nice meal when you get back," Debbie said on the phone. "What would you like?"

"Meat! Don't care what it is, just meat!"

That's really nice of her. She's so sweet. She's . . .

"Hang on! Why?"

"Why what?"

"Why the nice meal?"

"Because I love you, and I want you to be happy. And I've arranged for you to take the turkeys and the geese and help with the plucking and I know you're not going to like it and I'm really sorry. Are you still there?"

I hadn't even made it home and we were already planning what to kill next.

"Oh," was all I managed.

"You don't have to help with the plucking, only if you don't, they said they haven't got time to do ours until after Christmas, so it's kind of important that you do. If you can. But you don't have to decide yet. What do you think?"

On second thoughts, forget being excited about going home.

The day after I got back from London, I loaded every single turkey into the trailer and drove them off to be killed. As I drove down the twisty, turny country lanes, I couldn't help wondering what makes me any better than a fox, and whether at the end of the day, when all the turkeys were dead and hanging up, I'd want to grind my own face into the mud?

I didn't see the turkeys being killed, but stood in a line of guys and teenage girls, mostly eastern European but some old-boy farmers there, too, and together we plucked. And plucked. And plucked. In a way, it was good that I was in a group as when my 40 turkeys came through — I couldn't miss them, mine were bronze

119

traditional types as opposed to the standard white ones everyone else had — I couldn't get upset. The others were really kind and gave me lots of thumbs up and appreciative nods.

"You left a turkey behind," Debbie said when I got home.

"I did? I'll take it tomorrow." I was due back the following day with the geese.

The following morning we both went down onto the land to load the geese and the final turkey. I got the trailer hitched to the truck and positioned Debbie at the back.

"I'll grab a goose and put it in," I said, explaining my action plan. "You open and close the door behind me, okay?"

She nodded.

I grabbed a goose and put it in. It was the male and he went potty, screaming for his woman: geese mate for life and this was the first time he'd ever been out of sight from his partner.

I went off to get the other goose. When I got back to the trailer, Debbie was standing there with tears streaming down her cheeks. I knew how she felt. I set the goose down, opened the door and let the other one free. They waddled away together like two fat ladies with wet knickers on.

"How much had we sold them for?" I asked.

"A lot of money."

"Well, don't blame me when we're broke and can't afford to feed ourselves." Secretly, I'd put up with not being able to feed ourselves if only I didn't have to take anything else to be killed.

"What about the turkey?" Debbie said.

"Boy or girl?" I asked.

"Girl."

"Lucky-Turkey-Leaky. Why don't we get some more chickens and she can live with them?"

"I didn't think you liked chickens?" She was smiling, knowing how I really felt about them.

"I don't. Stupid things. Can't stand them."

She nodded. "I know you don't. You're just doing it for me."

I waved my hand in a motion through the air that said, I'm all heart.

CHAPTER
FIFTEEN

We'd been on Exmoor for a little over three years, and although this was to be our fourth Christmas in the cottage, it felt special because this was the first one we'd immersed ourselves in the country ways and not simply recreated the type of Christmas we had in London with a fake tree smothered in gaudy tinsel.

Christmas came just at the point when money was getting tight, though there was never a question over a lavish Christmas dinner because just about everything was home-made or home reared. The home-grown turkey was golden and moist. There was bacon on top that was home cured, succulent sausage meat and honey-glazed ham — there were probably vegetables, too, but — man alive — for a passionate meat eater, this was a meaty Christmas orgasm of a feast. I chopped wood for the fire, cut holly and ivy for Debbie to decorate the windowsills that she intertwined with tiny white fairy lights. The tree in the corner was real and smelled of pine, and we hung red beads and white lights, pinecones and ribbons tied in bows to make it look pretty. And it did. It looked stunning.

There were whole oranges studded with cloves hanging around the walls and slices of dried orange sticking out of wooden bowls filled with nuts. There were candles everywhere. It was beautiful.

On Christmas Eve, Debbie and I walked hand in hand through our woods until we found a real yule log (before they became chocolate-coated Swiss rolls, yule logs were an ancient pagan tradition) that we took home. As it got dark, we turned off all the lights in the house and burnt it in the fire for good luck.

The build-up to Christmas had been manic, and although we made money on the turkeys sending them around the country, we lost a fortune on the geese because we had to source and buy two free-range oven-ready geese at vast expense to fulfil the orders, while ours continued to waddle happily around the field. So it wasn't until a few days after the festivities that I managed to test out my aggressive and passive theory on the pigs.

It was a bitterly cold day. Wrapped up in so many layers, I moved with less grace than Frankenstein's monster. I shuffled onto the quad bike, called Dex up behind me and drove down onto the land.

The evening rounds of feeding, watering and bedding down took a couple of hours. I started with the poultry and put them to bed, and by the time I moved on to the pigs, I was warm enough to shed some of the layers, making me look a little more human.

I walked down to the edge of the enclosure in the woods and tossed in the food as usual. When it is dry, I like to spread out their food on the ground as it seems more natural for them to root about for their dinner as that's how they'd eat in the wild. Then I stood back and composed myself. I dropped my shoulders, bent a little forward, smiled and went in sideways looking a lot like a drunk tramp on a Friday-night binge.

The pigs knew I was there, some of them even came over to me to sniff before scampering back to the food, but none of them made any real approach.

Success! Something I'd done, something I'd figured out myself actually worked. Keeping my composure, I went over to the pigs and started stroking them. They felt freezing.

I went back up to the house and banged on the door.

"What's happened?" Debbie said, opening up in a fluster.

"Nothing. I need your help. The pigs are cold. I thought we'd barbecue some potatoes and give them a little hot snack. What do you think?"

She considered me for a while, head slightly on one side. "You're mad," she said, laughing, then added, "Okay."

And that's what we did. We barbecued jacket potatoes and then sneaked into each of their houses to share them out. In fact, they weren't particularly cold snuggled up together in the deep straw beds of their houses, but they loved the snack attack.

I saved the biggest and best potato for Kylie, feeding it to her while she lay in bed, picking up all the little bits that she dropped and popping them back into her mouth.

We should get more pigs. Lots more pigs.

After Christmas it was hard to go back to work. If December is the quietest month for estate agents,

January is the busiest. Everyone, it seems, sits around over the festive period and decides to move. The influx of property onto the market in the first few weeks of the New Year is staggering.

So I'm back in London early January missing home. I miss my animals. I keep thinking of Kylie and Dex and my horse Bobby. London is grey, I mean really grey. There's just no green here at all. At night, I drink wine and watch TV, but it doesn't feel as comfortable as it used to. Debbie offers to make me food parcels of our own meat, but I keep refusing. I don't want to recreate home in London, it wouldn't feel right. So I eat lots of fish and vegetarian ready meals, which makes me sad. I still love London with the same intensity I always have; I just don't feel as though I need it quite as much as I used to.

I drink too much wine and eat a gloomy meal for one with aubergines in it — who, in their own sober mind, ever eats aubergines? Nobody in the history of the planet has ever said, "Ooh, I *really* fancy a nice aubergine now."

I stagger up to the bedroom in my mum's house and lie on the bed, staring up at the ceiling, thinking about the animals. It's cold out, and I hope Kylie's babies are okay. I hope Bobby is warm enough in her stable. I worry about the sheep. I worry about Dex. I really think we should get some more chickens soon. And finally, I drift off to sleep.

The phone rings at 2 am.

It's a bit of a shock.

Unless you're lucky enough to be newly in love, under 18 or some sort of night worker, there is no dread deeper than the 2 a.m. phone call. Good news does not come at 2 am. That's the bad-news hour, with conversations that start, "I'm sorry" or "I don't want to worry you, but . . ."

I blinked at the mobile in my hand without even remembering reaching for it. The word "Debbie" shone out in the darkness, and some idiotic ringtone sing-songed in the silence. I pressed the green button, noting the time and feeling an iceberg form in the pit of my stomach.

"Darcy's escaped," Debbie said.

Fumbling about on the bedside table for the nightlight, I sent my mother's spare-room pictures and knick-knacks tumbling to the floor before I found the switch. "Okay, that's not a problem," I said.

"Yes, yes, it is a problem. Did you hear me, Darcy's escaped?" Darcy, 12-stone of lolloping Great Dane dog and the world's biggest baby. Untrainable, unpractical, unintelligent and utterly adorable.

"Where are you?"

"On the land, just walking past Kylie's enclosure. I think she's asleep. Does that mean Darcy hasn't been past here? Oh, I think I might have woken her up. Hello, sweetie." I could hear the pig snorting and snuffling in the background and imagined Debbie shining a torch into her face. Yep, that'd wake her up.

"Darcy!" she yelled. I did that stupid pull-the-phone-away-from-my-ear-and-stare-at-it-rudely thing. Then I

126

lifted it back. "Can't you shout quietly? Or at least move the phone when you do."

"Sorry. What am I going to do? I can't see him anywhere. It's not so bad if he's contained on our land, but what if he gets out? You know how soppy he is."

Actually, I was more concerned he might get tangled up in one of the electric fences or find himself face to face with the pigs in the woods.

"I think he must have gone out the end path. I bet there's a bitch in season somewhere in Barbrook and he's gone after her," she said. "The thing is, I'm not sure I can go out there."

"Why not?"

"I was in bed. Darcy said he needed to go to the loo and it was urgent. I wasn't expecting to go traipsing through the streets." She sighed, "I'm only wearing wellies and a long coat."

I started laughing. "You're joking?"

Silence.

"What, nothing? Nothing under the coat at all?"

"Shut up," she said, but with a smile in her voice.

I laughed even harder. Then I put on a mock stern voice, "Mr Dawson, we've arrested your wife for streaking through the village."

"I'm not streaking, I'm decent. I'm just not fully decent. Besides it's two in the morning, who's going to know? Oh, damn it, I'm going to have to go out and find him. Hang on."

The sound of her footsteps changed to a slap-slap sound. I guessed she was now off the land and walking along the pavement. "Isn't it a bit chilly?" I asked.

"Don't. Wait. I think I've seen him. Yes, oh no, he's in the petrol station." Then very quietly, almost a whisper, she called, "Darcy, here, boy."

"Where are you?"

"Sssh. Hiding behind a bush. Darcy, come to mummy."

"But the petrol station's closed."

"They don't turn off the lights, and I bet there's CCTV or something. Darcy, please, for me, please, come . . . Got him!"

"Better?"

"Simon, it's two in the morning, I'm nearly naked, walking the streets, freezing cold, with a dog that thinks I've come out to play. Do I feel better? Better than what, exactly?"

I laughed and switched off the phone. Better than me stuck in London, I thought.

I spent the rest of the winter alternating between Exmoor and London. I knew I was drinking too much in London, but I told myself it was to hide the disgusting vegetarian ready meals I was eating. It might even have been true. Maybe partly true anyway. I worked all week and lived for the weekend when I could go home.

It's hard to get much done over a short weekend when most of the time is taken up riding Bobby and Georgie, playing with Dex and talking to the pigs, but I tried to get some work done on the land.

In early spring, we bought more chickens. It's amazing how much I'd missed having them around. I called Ziggy and told him, and he insisted on coming back with me for the weekend. I picked him up on the way home.

"So what have you ruined without me?" he demanded, putting his rucksack in the back of the car and launching a carrier of beer into the front footwell before sitting in the passenger seat and cracking open a can.

"It's a five-hour journey, you'll be bombed by the time we get back."

"I bloody well hope so!"

"Yeah, well, just don't spill any."

"Are you going to be this grumpy all the way?"

"Sorry. 'Course not."

"What's up?" He took a sip as I edged the car out into the Friday afternoon traffic. "You can't still be frustrated at leaving London to go to your country residence for the weekend."

"I'm not. I think it's the other way around."

"You mean you want to be there and not in London now?" He laughed.

I nodded.

"Inevitable. Hang on, then why are you in a bad mood if that's where we're going?"

I shrugged. "I don't know."

It's one thing not wanting to be in London, but it's another not wanting to not want to be in London. Put it another way, I didn't want to be in London, but I still wanted to want to be there. As crazy as it sounds, I think I missed missing London.

I told Ziggy. He nodded. But we didn't dwell on in and spent the remainder of the journey going over a small section of his love life. A very small part of it. And I thought *my* life was complicated . . .

The following morning I was up and out before anyone else had even stirred. It wasn't even daylight. I went to the barn and had a 10-minute fuss-up with Dex, and walked him up to the horses rather than drive the quad. For someone who hated being outside, I was pretty happy.

I groomed Bobby, then I groomed Georgie, then I groomed Bobby again. I've never had a confidante, my thoughts never seem ordered enough to articulate to anyone outside of my own head. But horses don't care if you make sense or not. So I opened up and told Bobby everything. I told her all my worries and fears about how I felt about London, home and my place in it all. It felt good to get it all out, even if she did fall asleep through most of it.

Then I tacked up Georgie and hopped on her back. When it was just about light, I walked her out onto Ilkerton Ridge, warming her up until she felt free and loose and was really listening to me. I collected her by shortening the reins so she couldn't go forward, sat deep and squeezed her with my knees just enough to get her back end right underneath her, and at that point I pushed myself up out of the saddle, tapped her with my legs and released the reins. She sprang forward, going from standstill to 20 miles an hour in three strides. It was a beautiful feeling as we galloped over the moorland, me urging her on, her whole body working in a rhythmic backward-and-forward motion as her muscles pounded, driving us faster and faster and faster, my head low down right up her neck, my bodyweight all the way forward.

Exmoor is an incredible place to ride. We galloped through knee-high bracken, jumped ditches and finished with a hill climb so steep I had to put my arms around her neck to stop myself falling off backwards. At the top, we stopped to catch our breath, both panting but exhilarated. The view was breathtaking, nothing but open moorland in every direction and from there we watched the sun peeking above the horizon. I dropped the reins so they looped down and walked home, steering with tiny shifts in my bodyweight.

By the time we got back, she was cool and calm. I put headcollars on both horses and led them out into the field to turn them loose. Then I walked back down the hill, jumped onto the quad bike and drove onto our land.

CHAPTER
SIXTEEN

The sun was up and it was a beautiful morning. I sidled in with Kylie and gave her and her babies their breakfast. Then I let out the chickens along with the rest of the poultry — the new cockerel was White, a good-looking boy but nothing like Red. White was more your once-on-a-Saturday-night-missionary-position-if-you-please type of guy. But the hens seemed to like him, probably because they'd never met Red and didn't know what they were missing.

I fed the pigs in the woods and got a bucket of water from the stream to give them a drink. I was lost in my own world, and a very nice world it was, too. I didn't feel old, I didn't feel fat, I didn't feel frumpy — just some of the stresses I tend to negotiate on an average day in London. I felt good. I had a spring in my step, and when I reached a five-bar gate that needed climbing in order to get to the pigs, I hopped halfway up with no trouble at all. Lifting and steadying the bucket of water on the top rung, I swung a leg up and over so I was straddling the gate.

Just as I was about to bring my other leg over, my foot slipped. It slipped through the bars. I toppled forward, my back leg hooking over the top bar, my front leg caught between the bars further down so I was doing the splits through the rungs of the gate. The rest of my body somersaulted until I was upside down, my head a couple of inches from the ground, my feet still trapped. Then I poured the entire contents of the bucket of water into my own face.

I nearly drowned. Half went up my nose, half went in my shocked open mouth. I couldn't breathe. I thought I was going to die, drown hung up and upside down on a gate in the middle of a field.

I had flash images of years to come where people would tentatively ask of Debbie, "How did your husband die?" and she'd have to admit, "He tied himself to a gate with his own limbs and then drowned by pouring a bucket of water up his nose." Nobody should have to go through life like that.

I really should keep a tally of these near-death experiences. That's what, four? Five? Maybe I should stop with the list of animals that replays itself over and over again in my head and start a new one of near-death experiences — talking of which:

Georgie and Bobby

Kylie and her eight teenage hooligans

A mob of pigs in the woods

Dex, my gorgeous, one-eyed puppy

Darcy

Sheep

Ducks

Lucky-Turkey-Leaky

Two killer geese

Chickens

White, the cockerel

That's quite a list for someone who still half lives in London.

But I didn't die on the gate. I spluttered and, for a while, I thought it was touch and go, but I didn't die. But a few months later when I took the first of Kylie's babies to slaughter, part of me wished I hadn't made it after all.

God, where do you start on that one, except to say that at some point I myself am going to die and will probably be pulled into some side room and asked to account for the actions of my life. What am I going to say? Sorry? Whoops?

I'll say: "I looked after the pigs and gave them a great life in which they were happy, and I kept them as long as I could."

He'll say: "I wasn't going to ask you about that, but seeing as you brought up the subject . . ."

I'll say: "That's not fair, what bit did *you* want me to account for?"

He'll say: "No, no, tell me about the pigs."

I'll say: "Damn. Okay, I reared pigs and they trusted me and loved me and then I sent them to be killed and then I ate them."

He'll say: "That's not very nice. Why did you do that?"

I'll say: "Because . . . Because I didn't want to eat meat from animals that weren't happy."

He'll say: "Haven't you heard of vegetarianism?"

I'll say: "But it doesn't work that way."

134

He'll say: "Yes, it does. We sent you enough warnings with the near-death experiences. Didn't that give you a clue?"

I'll say: "That was *you*?"

He'll say: "You should have seen your face when you electrocuted your testicles. We laughed for weeks over that one."

I'll say: "And when I got hung up on the gate and poured a bucket of water over my head and nearly drowned?"

He'll say: "No, Simon. That one was all you."

Or what if it's not a person who asks me to account for my actions but the pigs themselves? All the pigs that I've sent off, all waiting for me. What would I say then? Jesus, I can't think about that.

"How do you feel about all this?" I asked Debbie, not entirely off topic as we were chopping one of Kylie's baby's into handy-size joints and popping them in bags before fitting them into the freezer.

"I hate sending them off. I *really* hate sending them off. But this bit I absolutely love, and I'm so proud of what we do. Only eating our own meat that's been happy and has been well looked after is a good thing. And the flavour is stunning. How about you, how do you feel?"

"Oh, you know, the same." I think in lots of ways I did feel the same, only perhaps I wasn't as far down the road as she was.

"I think we should get more pigs," I said.

"More? How many more?"

"A couple more sows and a boar. We need a male. We need to breed."

I think I felt the same as I had with Kylie — that need for some sort of balance, to create life as well as take it away. So we did. We bought two more sows and a boar.

The boy is wonderful. A Berkshire boar with kind eyes and a squat nose, ears that stood up so he looked alert, bright and intelligent, and four white socks, one on each of his hoofs.

"What are we going to call him?" Debbie asked.

I'd recently had a male moment and been watching some testosterone TV, *The Top One Hundred Coolest Cars On TV* or something. I had probably spent the day caring for the animals and felt the need to touch base with my masculinity even though I normally avoid programmes like that. Anyway, the top coolest car was the General Lee from *The Dukes of Hazard*, and I thought, what a great name for a pig!

I told Debbie.

"The General Lee, I could live with that," she said.

I made more enclosures and built more houses for all the different sets of pigs, and it felt like a community, and acted like one, too. There were arguments and fights between the pigs. There was sex and love, friendships, falling out and making up. It was a porcine soap opera that changed every day, and I loved it. Each night, I hauled heavy sacks of feed and buckets of water about to give them food and drink, and caught up with the latest. Then I'd go home hot and sweaty and full of gossip.

"Go and have a bath, will you? Dinner's nearly ready," Debbie said.

"But I haven't told you about —"

"Later. Bath first."

I lay in the bath. It's true estate agents don't get a great deal of exercise and I could see my body changing. The muscles in my arms were firming nicely, but other things were changing, too. My pecs were twice the size they used to be, and now I could almost fill a small-cup bra. And from the horse riding my waist was slimmer, but my hips wider, and my bum was fleshier.

Hang on! I leapt out of the bath and went storming downstairs.

"Hel-*lo*, baby," Debbie said, not even mentioning the fact that I was naked and hadn't towelled off, was dribbling bath water all over the carpet.

"Don't hello bloody baby me. Look! *Look at me!*"

"Yep, I am."

"Well, don't you see?"

"Oh yes."

"Debbie! Don't you see what's happening?"

"What's happening? What are you on about?"

I pointed out the changes. "I'm developing breasts, wide slim hips and a fleshy bum."

"So?"

"So all this farm work and caring for animals and horse riding rubbish is turning me into a woman! I don't want to be a woman!"

"I think you'll find you're just not used to being fit. I also think you'll find it takes a bit more to make a woman, and *that* certainly isn't feminine."

"You're sure?" I said, following her gaze and looking down.

"I'm sure."

"Okay." I went back up.

Later she said, "I thought you were going to jump on me when you came down all wet earlier. It was very erotic."

"Was it?"

"Don't you fancy me anymore?" she said.

"Of course I do."

"I wouldn't blame you if you didn't. I never get to dress up anymore. I'm never out of wellies. I feel drab. I don't feel sexy."

"Of course I fancy you, I just had other things on my mind, that's all. It's odd when you don't recognise your own body, you know."

"I don't always recognise me these days," she said.

"That's okay, I recognise you," I said helpfully.

"Gee, thanks."

"I didn't mean it like that."

The next night, when we were down doing the pigs and watching the General strut his funky stuff with one of the ladies, I took her in my arms and kissed her, not just a peck, but properly. When we broke away, she looked flustered and said, "Don't. I look awful. You shouldn't be doing things like that."

"Why not?"

"Because," she said, grabbed me and we did it again, our four feet planted in wellies sinking in the squishy mud. I worked it out that other than a quick nip into town for shopping, we hadn't been out together for nearly six months. I had London where I could dress up. She didn't. I felt sorry for her and decided to take her out as soon as possible. Somewhere nice. Somewhere where she would be happy. Somewhere that sold happy food. Or a happy meal. Somewhere where we could go large if we wanted to . . .

"I am not going to bloody McDonalds!"

"I said that out loud, didn't I?"

"Yes, you did!"

She stormed off.

I'd have to watch that.

In the meantime, the General was getting all the sows pregnant, and all the sheep had been covered by the ram. The chickens were at it day and night. The ducks were bonking, the geese banging. Seriously, you have no idea how much sex is going on in the countryside. It's one enormous orgy.

It's not all lovey-dovey sex either. Some of it's kind of kinky. I watched two ducks chase and catch a chicken. One held her down, while the other jumped on her and did the biz, then they changed places. When they'd finished, she pretended to run off. I'm not being a man about this and say she "pretended" to run off: she really did pretend to run off, and when the ducks made only a half-hearted attempt to catch her again, she purposely tripped over in front of them so they tumbled on top of her. I've seen pigs perform oral sex. I didn't know where to look! And they're not like humans caught in an intimate act who will try and hide what they were doing, oh no, they just carry on regardless.

139

Which means everything got pregnant (on this we can assume the oral sex was just porcine foreplay). Which means everything needed a midwife. Me! I became the midwife. I cut my nails, scrubbed my hands and perfected my bedside manner with an, "Excuse me, madam, lie still, deep breath, I'm just going to have a rummage."

After nearly vomitting over the chick hatching between Debbie's boobs, I was now pulling out babies. One time, I was attending to a sow, kneeling down at the sharp end and talking her through the procedure so that she'd be aware that I knew what I was on about, when Debbie said, "Are you okay if I go off for a while?"

"Sure. Where are you going?"

"I want to check the oil and water in the car. I meant to do it earlier, but completely forgot. I know they're low and want to get it sorted while I've got a minute."

So she went off and serviced the car while I delivered eight bouncing baby piglets. At the time, it didn't seem odd. Afterwards, lying in bed that night, deconstructing the day, it struck me that maybe I was losing my masculine role in all of this. Not that I could've serviced the car even if you paid me. I've always had company cars and haven't got a clue about engines, but it's such a male thing to do, open the bonnet and tinker, that I somehow felt a lesser man: not only was my wife doing it, but I was delivering babies while she did. This thought got to me so much that I got up and wandered around the house in the middle of the night, looking for something macho and blokey to do in order to re-establish our "his" and "hers" roles in my head. I thought of putting on some porn so she could catch me watching it, but I could hear her snoring upstairs so that was no good. In the end, I switched on the TV, aiming to find a car programme or a "game", but instead found a programme about dressmaking and crochet — just kidding. No, truth is, I couldn't find anything worth watching, so I went back to bed feeling pretty wretched and not wondering where all this was heading. I could see where it was heading, but wondering where I was going within it all because I really liked delivering the babies, I *really* liked delivering the babies. So why did that make me feel so bad?

CHAPTER
SEVENTEEN

In the morning, I got up and went out to check on my piglet team that I'd delivered while Debbie was playing mechanic with our car. The first 24 hours are crucial as the piglets need to take on enough colostrum (the rich, first-stage milk) from their mum. They also shouldn't get too cold, lost, squashed or anything like that.

I peeked in. I could see mum and I could see a clump of piglets snuggled up beside her, but I could also see a couple separate, lying still in the straw. I crawled in and made my way over to them. They were dead. Squashed. I picked them up and took them outside.

It happens. Some mums are really good; others are just clumsy. I sat cross-legged in the dirt with the still babies in my lap. I stroked them. They felt cold. I told them I was sorry and I told them they'd be missed. I wanted to . . . Oh, I don't know. It's so stupid. They'd gone through all of that, been conceived, grown, the miracle of birth, just to die. Why? It's the same as the chick that hatched between Debbie's boobs. What a waste, what a stupid, stupid waste. I know it's crazy, but what I really wanted to do was complain to someone. I wanted to bang on someone's door and yell, "Are you in charge here? 'Cos this is a bloody disgrace, now *sort it out!*"

I put the dead babies in a bag.

At lunchtime, two more were dead.

"We've got a problem here," I said to Debbie. "That's four babies she's squashed. Surely that's more than just clumsiness? Clumsiness is tripping over and knocking into things, not killing half your children."

Debbie agreed. They had plenty of room, but a baby's urge is to be close to its mother, and if that mother rolls over without much care, well, you can see how it happens. I thought of taking the piglets away and hand-rearing them for a while, but that's fraught with just as many dangers and the success rate is poor. All I could do was keep extra vigilant and nip back as often as I could.

By evening, we were really in trouble. She'd killed two more, and it was now apparent that she was killing them with intent rather than by accident. Whether she knew what she was doing, that she was murdering her own children, I don't know. But I think she must have an awareness of it to some extent as it was all deliberate. We had no choice. I had to get the remaining two piglets out of there.

I went in, but I was too late for one of them. That left one poor little scared piglet. I tried to get it, but it kept running away from me and back to mum. I tried getting mum out of the way. I tried tempting her with food. I tried getting a sheet of wood as a barrier between her and the baby. The baby was crying, mum was stressed, and I was making things worse. Equally, I knew I had to do something, I couldn't just sit there and watch her kill that one, too. Then mum turned her attention away from me and onto the baby. She started chasing it around, trying to squash it with her head against the wall.

I could see what was happening. I had to act quickly. I went in with knees, fists and slaps and screamed at the top of my voice — I didn't know what the hell else to do! Body language and conversing with pigs is fine, but this was way beyond that. I screamed and slapped her back and sides and lunged for the baby, but she was so much bigger than me and turned her body, so I fell, banging my shoulder hard.

Pain exploded. I got to my knees, aiming to have one final go, but it was too late. The situation was out of control. Mum caught the piglet and drove it against the wall. The piglet screamed a high-pitched squeal, screamed and screamed, then went quiet.

Mum turned and walked away.

I stared at the poor little mite. My arm throbbed, and I clutched it with the other hand. It felt broken, but no more broken than the rest of me because all of me felt smashed. I lay down in the straw. I should have done things differently. I should have reacted earlier. I shouldn't have lost it screaming and lashing out like that, what the hell did I think I was doing? But I did the only thing that seemed right at the time.

I'm no farmer, I'm a stupid estate agent. I'm just playing at this, and now I'm wrecking things and causing death.

Eight babies dead. Eight babies dead. Eight babies dead. I chanted it in my head. I wanted to blame myself, like I'd done something wrong, but I didn't know what else I could have done to change the situation.

"You didn't do anything wrong," Brian the pig man said.

I'd gone straight home, phoned him and said that I had a sow for him to take away. "I don't care what you do with it — I don't want to know what you do with it — I just need it gone," I'd said.

He was there within an hour.

"You get some that are like that. Her's just not a good mother," he said.

Yeah, that's something of an understatement. We loaded her, and I didn't watch her leave.

That evening, I did the rounds feeling heavy and sluggish. My arm wasn't broken; it only hurt. That wasn't why I was heavy and sluggish, though. I was heavy and sluggish because any ounce of enthusiasm and energy I had for all this farm malarkey was gone.

I fed, watered and checked on everyone because I had to. I didn't talk to Kylie, I didn't talk to the General in my language or theirs, I just did what I had to do. When I came to the pens with the new mothers and their babies, I made myself hang around to watch, even though I wanted to run away with my fingers in my ears, singing la-la-la-la-la!

In one pen there was a piglet off to one side. I can't handle it again, I thought. But you have to. I jumped in and picked it up. It wasn't dead. Thank God for that. I took it outside. It was cold and shivery. I hugged it close for a while, wondering what to do, when it sneezed. That made up my mind. I took off my fleece top and tied the piglet into it by knotting the arms, then I propped it between my legs on the seat of the quad bike and drove it up to the house.

"Is this the cottage hospital?" I called out in as light a voice as I could muster, carrying the piglet into the kitchen. "Don't panic, it's not happened again. It's just that this little one's not feeling too good right now and needs a room for the night."

CHAPTER
EIGHTEEN

The last episode in a brilliant TV series is on the television. The revelation, the bit that ties all the strands together in clever ways I couldn't possibly imagine — or at least, that's what I think is going on because I can't hear it. The volume is switched to mute.

I want to tell Debbie this is crazy, but I can't because we're being quiet so the poorly piglet can get some sleep. She's snuggled up in the wicker log basket on a mound of soft fluffy towels in front of a blazing log fire, snoring — the piglet, not Debbie.

Debbie's next to me, grinning. I can *hear* her grinning. It's almost louder than the piglet's snoring. Then she turns to me and gives me a "Shush". I haven't said anything. What's she shushing me for?

"You were going to say something," she whispers.

"That's so unfair —" she stops me with a finger across my lips, then turns it into an affectionate stroke on my cheek. I huff. I know it's childish, but breathing is the only form of noise I'm allowed to make. I huff again, louder, but she's ignoring me. So I start to fidget, I can't help it, doing this little foot dance thing in the air while I sit on the sofa.

The piglet is racking up some volume now, alternating between snoring and farting, popping and banging like an old sports car. I have the urge to go over to the basket and pinch her nose, and suddenly this strikes me as the funniest thing I have ever thought of in my life. I have to bite my finger hard to stop the laugh from bursting out.

I catch Debbie's eye, and suddenly we're both biting our fingers trying not to laugh. I feel like a naughty schoolboy in the back of the classroom. You have no idea how difficult it is to remain quiet, still and straight-faced when you're told that's what you have to do, even when the person telling you is the one trying not to break the rules alongside you.

In the morning, the piglet demonstrates she's feeling a lot better by decorating the lounge carpet with plenty of poo and pee. You know you can walk into a house and tell by tasting the air if the owners have ever had a baby? Well, I'm paranoid someone in days or years to come is going to walk in here and say, "Do you keep pigs in the house?"

The piglet, not looking as though she's ever had a day's sickness in her entire life, is playing a game of dashing at dizzying speed around the sofa, squeaking happily.

I'm grumpy. It's early morning, I haven't had a coffee, and my lounge is a pig's toilet, so I do the sod-off sound, and the piglet does it back! Honestly, the youth of today.

Figuring the little thing must now be empty, I leave her to her run-around game and start clearing up, which involves calling up the stairs to Debbie that there's a bodily fluids emergency and I can't tackle it without honking up everywhere, so could she please come down and help? I go into the kitchen, make coffee and assist by throwing plastic bags, rolls of paper towel and bottles of cleaning fluid into the lounge and calling directions. If I'm honest, it's not a great way to start the day for any of us. Except maybe the piglet.

My real trouble comes a bit later. How to get a wriggling, lively piglet back down to her mum and brothers and sisters on the quad bike? When I brought her up, she was ill and still. Now she's well and a bouncing baby hooligan. But I have a cunning plan. If I tuck my fleece top into my jeans, put on a belt and pull it tight, then put the piglet down inside, I could drive down the hill. Would that work? It's worth a try.

I carry the piglet to the bike and climb on. Then I open up the neck of my top and poke the piglet down. She squeals, gets caught up in the material and kicks out ferociously. Her little trotters are like daggers in my tummy. Now we're both squealing, and my jumper is flipping somersaults. I grit my teeth, turn on the bike and drive off.

Everything is fine until halfway down the hill when she manages to stick a foot through the fleece and rip a hole. But rather than try to escape, she pokes her head out of the gap and calms down, watching the world go by.

The only awkward moment came when a car crammed full of cases and bags, quilts and pillows, and lots of very tired-looking people, tried to get past me on the lane. It's a single track and space is tight, so we both slowed down to inch by. I smile and so does the piglet. As we drive off, I can hear them yelling, "He's got a pig sticking out of his front!"

I tell Debbie about it when I go back up, having dropped off the piglet first. I had watched as she dashed into the piggy mix of her brothers and sisters, until I couldn't tell which one she was, which was a good sign considering how ill she looked yesterday.

"You don't think we've turned eccentric, do you?" I asked, giving the kettle a wobble to see if there was water in it.

Debbie smiled. "I don't think so," she said.

"You're sure?"

"I'm sure. It's not like you to drive up and down the hill with a piglet stuffed down your front all the time, is it? It's just a one-off. One-offs don't make you eccentric, they just mean you're having an interesting day, that's all."

"I don't want to be eccentric."

"I know you don't. And you're not. So that's okay then." She turned away and carried on making breakfast.

I didn't really want to drop the subject, but what more could I say? I hated the thought of anyone thinking I was weird.

"I'm going to get ready," I said.

"Ready for what?"

"For the day."

"But you are, aren't you?"

"No. Not really."

150

Walking upstairs I found a smart pair of jeans and a casual top. I changed into them, cramming my work gear in a plastic bag and tying the top so it wouldn't pong out the bedroom. Then I put on a pair of new white trainers.

"Where are you going?" Debbie said when I came back down.

"Onto the land. Stafford said he'd come over and give me a few tips on using the chainsaw. I think he's worried I might cut off a leg."

"Dressed like that?"

"I just feel better like this. I'll be careful and I won't get dirty." Even I knew that was a crazy thing to say, but she didn't argue.

Most people down here have at least two jobs. The postman is also the window cleaner. The butcher cleans the public toilet on his way home from a day's butchery. If you want your chimney swept, the post office is the place to go. The mechanic at the garage in Lynton is the local cabby, and Stafford, the publican of the local pub, is also a tree surgeon.

I ate breakfast and then went back down onto the land. Stafford met me there. Early 60s, with wild eyebrow hair almost as long as the greying, curly hair on his head, Stafford was a man with a story for every occasion, and an occasion for every story. And then another story. In fact, it was rumoured that the only way to stop him telling stories was to sit him down because he was incapable of talking without punctuating everything by stepping backward one pace at the end of every dramatic sentence, only to step forward again at the beginning of the next. At the end of an anecdote he would roar with laughter and go for a little walk up and down and in tight little circles in front of you. It must be something to do with spending so much time behind the bar.

"Stafford," I called.

He took a step back (I swear he was already halfway through a story even without anyone else there to listen). I'd made a few friends since we'd been down, but Stafford was without doubt the best of them, and on that I wasn't alone: people talked about Stafford right across Devon, and on Facebook (he didn't do Twitter because you can't fit a good story into 140 characters) he had about a gazillion followers.

"Thanks for this," I said, holding out my hand and gripping his.

"Can't have you bloody townies coming down here and taking up beds in our hospitals with . . ." he did airborne speech marks with his fingers, something I haven't seen anyone else do for 20 years, ". . . tree-related injuries".

I called him a colourful version of a cheeky whatsit and he did his little walkabout bit in front of me, laughing. "Ooh, which reminds me of something —"

Just then, my phone went off. Saved by the bell, you might say. It was work. I held up an apologetic hand and moved a few feet away to take the call, not because I wanted to be in private, but because I was sure he'd carry on anyway. He did.

The estate agency where I work is owned by two people, a mother and a son. That is, my mother and her son — my brother. I work for my family, though I'm just an employee.

It was my mum on the phone.

She asked me how I was doing, and I told her that I was doing fine. I asked her how things in the office were, and she said that they were quiet, adding, "And that's why I phoned."

She told me things had been getting tougher, which I knew, and that she had to think of the profits and the staff. Then she dropped a bomb. "I don't need you next week," she said. "In fact, we'd like you to go part-time, which will be good for you because you've got the farm and it'll give you more time at home and we thought you'd be pleased. Anyway, someone's just come into the office, I've got to go," and she went. That was it.

I leaned against a tree. You know people say when they get bad news it feels as though they've been kicked in the stomach? Well, it's true. That's exactly how it feels.

"Staff, I'm sorry . . . I'm really sorry . . . I've got to go."

"Are you okay?" I've never seen him look so serious.

I quickly told him, then got on the bike and drove home up the hill.

"I knew you'd get dirty," Debbie said, watching me walk in and giving me a stern face. I kicked off the muddy trainers and told her what had happened.

"Oh no," she said.

"Yeah." We stood in the kitchen looking at each other, a tornado of thoughts — a tornado of the same thoughts — whipping through our minds. I was the one who voiced it. "Money's tight as it is. I don't know if we can survive with the income cut in half. The food bill for the animals alone is huge, and there's so much that needs doing on the land. Even if I do it myself, I've still got to buy materials. I just don't think we can do it."

"You want to give up?"

"What choice have we got? We've tried, but we can't survive on half wages."

"Can't you talk to them? Can't you explain the situation?"

I shook my head. "They're not like that. It wouldn't make any difference."

"What are we going to do?"

I didn't know what we were going to do. I forced myself to do a tally. I couldn't cope with individuals, just groups:

Horses

Chickens

Turkeys

Sheep

Pigs

Dogs

It had been seven years since we'd sold up in London and shifted our lives to Exmoor, and three years since we bought the land. That's a long enough time to collect things, and it just so happened that the things I'd collected were mouths to feed. Feeding mouths is expensive. Feed costs plenty, *plenty* of money. Probably a third of my wages went on animal food, which is a huge percentage even if we did get some of it back by selling some of the meat. Drop my wages in half and suddenly it's not a third going on animal feed, it's two-thirds of a much smaller pot with not enough left over to pay the bills.

Whatever way I looked at it, it didn't add up. The animals would have to go. But how could they? How could I sell Bobby? Or Dex? It would be like selling my best friends. Yet if I couldn't afford to feed them, what other choice did I have?

CHAPTER
NINETEEN

"We'll get jobs," I announced.

"We can try, but there aren't many around here, and the ones that are are minimum wage. That's no good to us because you'd have to leave London to work full-time down here and still earn less than you would working part-time in London. I can't get a job because who else is going to run the farm when you're away? No, I think the best we can do is build up the farm and make it into a success. This is our business. We can make it work."

Despite Debbie's optimistic view that we could make it work, I knew the farm would never be able to completely support us. On the other hand, the housing market might not always be so slow. If we could hang on for a few months, maybe things would get better and I could go full-time again. I knew, as business plans go, it was pretty rubbish, but I couldn't think of anything else to do.

Why was my life becoming dominated by things because I couldn't think of anything else to do? Since when had I become *that* passive?

I sat around for a week because I didn't have any money to do any work on the land and tried to come up with ideas that might make some cash. Then I went back to London.

I knew that if I got stroppy, I risked losing my job completely, so I went into the office acting like the happiest, busiest bunny on the planet. It was all an act. I hated it — not the work as such, but the pretence that surrounded it. I felt as though I had to be over-enthusiastic and over-positive until I became a caricature of myself, which is much harder work than just being yourself. It's draining using up all that energy smiling and being happy when what I wanted to do was scream at them, *I can't survive on half wages, give me back my full-time job!*

I thought I was holding together all the strands, and for ages I was, but one night it all came unravelled in a spectacular way. I think I was tired, I was stressed, I was confused over what to do for the best, and I was really, really worried. Not a great combo.

We were in a restaurant in Bluewater — mum, brother and brothers family. It was a meal out on the company, which we tended to do about once a week. I looked at the menu. The vegetarian options were boring, and everyone else was ordering really yummy, meaty dishes, so I asked the waiter if the meat was free range. He didn't know and said he'd find out. He wandered off and came back after a minute or so.

"Chef said it doesn't matter, free range doesn't affect the taste."

"No, it's not the taste I'm worried about. I'll only eat it if it's free range."

He shrugged and went off to find the manager. Clearly, I was marked as a problem customer.

The manager came over, a short dumpy man with a shiny head.

"What's the problem?" he asked, quite disinterested.

"It's no problem," I assured him. "It's just that I'd like to eat the meat, but I'll only eat it if it's free range."

He shrugged. "Makes no difference," he said.

"What makes no difference — I don't understand?"

"Free range, organic, it's all hype. Trust me, the chef is superb, this is the best meat you'll ever taste."

"Hype? You've got to be kidding, right?"

"Look, I know my business. There is absolutely no difference in taste."

"What about the animals? What about the way they've lived? What about their conditions?"

His eyebrows creased. "What about it? What difference does that make?"

Was it *me*? Was I asking something weird? Surely it made a difference; surely it made a *big* difference. I thought of Kylie at home mooching around her pen, lazing in the sun, chilling out. And then I switched the thought and imagined her in a cage, all cramped and sad. I felt angry, which I considered was a perfectly reasonable response to this foolish manager. Who wouldn't feel angry at him?

I wanted to tell him how wrong he was. I wanted to sit him down and go through it rationally, and calmly. But I couldn't because he'd wandered off. So I did the next best thing, picked up a glass of wine and hurled it at the bar. The manager stopped wandering and started running. I could hear the sudden silence grip the restaurant, everyone pushing their chairs back and ducking.

It felt surprisingly good, so I picked up a side plate and threw that, too. Then a huge waiter-cum-bouncer came over, threw me to the floor and sat on me.

The manager came back and started shouting at me.

My brother started shouting at me.

My mother started shouting at me.

They were all shouting at me.

This was not my proudest moment.

In hindsight, lying there, kissing the carpet with the wind forced out of my lungs by this brute sitting on me, I wondered if I might have overstepped the mark a touch. Just, you know, a touch.

It cost loads on mother's credit card before they'd let me get up.

Outside I said I was sorry, but now, rather than shout, nobody was talking to me at all.

That night, I lay in bed trying to figure out if there were any bits of me I still recognised. I am not the type of person to trash a restaurant, or maybe I am, but I never felt passionate enough to explode before. I didn't dislike this new version of me, this crockery-lobbing lunatic. I just didn't know him. Just as I wasn't sure I knew the environment which this stranger, me, now inhabited.

I no longer felt the way I used to about London. That much was clear. I no longer felt the way I used to about Devon either. They were both familiar and yet so unknown, like seeing a sudden and unexpected side to someone you believed you knew really well.

I went home at the end of my work stint, promising to pay back my mother, but knowing I didn't have the means, and not at all sure I'd have the means anytime soon. She didn't kiss me goodbye, and I felt I was becoming a stranger to her, too. It was a horrible thought.

CHAPTER
TWENTY

At home, I worked outside whenever there was light in the sky, and inside when there wasn't. Debbie and I both did. We shared the work, though I probably did more of the mucky work and Debbie did more of the inside work, which neither of us minded and seemed a fair divvy-up of the chores.

We were both utterly exhausted, and even my dreams that used to be full of aeroplane crashes now just consisted of me feeling tired and sleeping. I slept and dreamt of sleeping, and my dreaming self, in turn, dreamt of sleeping. It was like looking in one of those mirrors where you see yourself looking in a mirror, and in that mirror there you are again looking in a mirror, going on and on, getting smaller and smaller.

Things could have been a whole lot easier, and I would've had to work a whole lot less if I'd had the slightest clue what I was doing. Odd things didn't seem to work for me on the land. Things that should have been simple, should have been natural, weren't. Take fire. Man has been making fire for millions of years. There's no system, there's no logic, there's not even any theory. As a developing race we're way beyond all of that. You just get something dry that burns, set it alight and it goes whoosh. That's what fire does.

If only it was that simple.

I cleared paths, cut hedges and, with all the sticks, twigs and branches, built huge bonfires. Then I set light to them, and they burnt beautifully in the middle before fizzling out, leaving the main bulk of the bonfire untouched.

Even cavemen could make fire and they couldn't communicate with more than a grunt. And they didn't have matches, petrol or oil. I did, and I used the fuel liberally. Very liberally. I still couldn't get them to burn.

I should've gone for a pint with Stafford and asked him, or even given Brian a call, but I was too embarrassed. So I called Ziggy.

"You want me to come down and give you a hand?" he said.

"Sorry, can't afford you."

"What, my measly salary?"

I told him about losing half my London work.

"Bummer," he said, offering to come down anyway and work for nothing. It was a nice offer, but it wasn't just the money I gave him: it was the extra food, beer and everything else. We had to account for every penny now, so I said no.

"Okay, so tell me what you're doing with the fires."

I told him. Ziggy had gone through a druggy dark patch when he was young. Not full-blown addict, but a bit more than your normal pothead. As a sideline, when he was high, he became something of a pyromaniac, specialising in setting bus stops ablaze. The craze only lasted a few weeks before he got caught and cautioned. He now says that's what sparked his interest in the law, though that's unlikely to be true even if it did scare him off drugs and away from fires.

"You're building wigwams, right?" he said.

"Right."

Approaching him for advice on lighting a bonfire was a little like approaching David Beckham for help pumping up a football — on all matters of pyromania, Ziggy was naturally gifted.

"That's your problem. All you'll do is burn the heart out. When you build it, lay all the branches facing the same way on top of each other. That way, when it burns, it will collapse on itself and keep going."

Excuse me, eureka moment alert — oh yeah!

"And if that doesn't work," he added, "Use more petrol."

Not so eureka.

"I've got to remake all the mounds I want to burn then?" I asked.

"Not really. Just get a crowbar and knock them flat, that should do it."

Silence.

"You *have* got a crowbar," he said.

I have? Sure I have. Probably.

I found a metal bar with some kind of hook on the end that I guess is a crowbar, knocked the nice neat bonfires flat and set light to them. It worked. They burnt down to nothing. I had to be around to make sure the fire didn't spread, but I didn't have to watch them all the time, so I spent most of it with the pigs.

During this time, the General was negotiating adolescence and puberty en route to becoming a man, or at least a man-pig. There was so much he experienced that I recognised, so much that I had gone through, that I came to the conclusion that there is little fundamental difference between our natures.

I was there when he discovered girls and went all gawky and shy whenever he was around them. I watched him trying to make sense of his feelings, and I felt for him when he started showing off so the girls would notice him, even if they didn't seem to like what they were noticing.

I watched him chase after this one girly pig whom he idolised. He loved her with all his heart, but she didn't love him back and she wouldn't let him anywhere near her. In the end, he got so desperate to lose his virginity that he had to do it with anyone just for the sake of his sanity, so he started chasing anything in a, um, "skirt".

He became a man at 11 months old. Bless him, he was so happy! But his post-coital bliss lasted about 10 seconds before he decided that that really was very nice indeed, thank you very much, I'll have another go! And he did. And he did again, all afternoon. I felt oddly proud.

Something changed in him that day. I want to say he grew up, but it's not that. It's more like . . . he settled. Not settled with his surroundings, but settled with himself. Like he suddenly understood what all the confusing whirlwind of feelings was about and kind of accepted them for what they were. He still loved his favourite pretty pig, and she even started coming around to him once he stopped pestering her for sex all the time. Even though he would make love with the others, he would always return to her for cuddles and company afterwards, and she didn't seem to mind.

He quickly became an absolute whiz with the ladies. It was probably coincidence that it all happened around the time that Ziggy helped me figure out how to light the bonfires around the farm, but I reckon the romantic atmosphere created by the fires glowing orange and red in the dusk couldn't have gone unnoticed. It's the agricultural equivalent of candles in the bedroom.

The upshot of all this was lots of piggy babies. Luckily, word was spreading among our family and friends and we had a waiting market for the meat.

"We need to change what we're doing," Debbie said, head down over a leg of pork, tunnelling out the bone with a sharp knife. "Everyone wants chops and joints, which means there's so much else going to waste."

"What do you mean?" As far as I knew, it was only the yuck that was getting tossed away, things like the head, the tail and the feet.

"We make sausages, which means we have to skin the meat and throw that skin away. We should be making pork scratchings with it. And the head, we should be making brawn with that. We should be making faggots with the offal. We shouldn't be wasting anything. The next pig we do, I want to try doing things a little differently, if that's okay?"

Fine by me. It made me feel a little like I had with Black Bum and Spotty Bum, that need to eat every scrap, even the horrible bits, and I realised that that

165

feeling had never gone away. I became excited that we were going to use everything. It felt right. Better than it had since we started.

The first attempts at using everything were edible, but not great. It's all too easy to get the textures wrong, and while they might have a great flavour, you wouldn't be bowled over.

Over time, we learned the tricks of how to wow — which is to say, Debbie learned the tricks and I ate the results and went, wow! She would spend days lost in a whirl of cooking, watching cooking programmes on TV, reading cookery books and surfing cooking-related Internet sites until it bordered on obsession.

Of course I did nothing to stop her because this passion meant I was eating restaurant food every night. I admit that I encouraged her, but wouldn't you if your partner suddenly started knocking out Michelin Guide meals every dinnertime? We sold the prime joints and chops, and anything left Debbie would make into amazing old-fashioned meals. Meals my grandparents' great-grandparents would find familiar. But you can see why a lot of the dishes have fallen from favour because they're so labour intensive. Take brawn, made with the pig's head — it takes *two days*! We live in a world where you can forget anything that takes more than 20 minutes to cook. And yet here we were, making things that took two days.

Let me tell you, when you put that much time and effort into food, it changes the way you think. Sure, I used to scoff at collecting eggs, but living this life, if only part-time, I'd changed and could no more eat a battery-farmed egg than boil my own underwear and eat that. The struggle I had understanding why I couldn't eat meat away from home also became clearer. Lots of things became clearer. It was an enlightening time, which is unusual for me because mostly I seem to negotiate life by caking mud on all my ideas until I can't work out the terrain of any of my thoughts.

The reason I figured I couldn't eat meat away from home was because, without any conscious input, I had developed this annoying habit: every time I ate meat, I thought about how that animal had lived. It made me acutely aware of what I was eating, at times even ruinously aware, which, on the whole, I considered to be a good thing. It didn't make me a popular dinner guest, though. That, and the fact that I had gained a reputation for chucking around the crockery.

While I still struggle, and probably always will, with the thought of killing my animals to eat them, I was comfortable that while they were alive they did lead happy, natural lives. That's important. And because I could only guess at the conditions mass-produced meat is reared in, I couldn't eat it. Right now, that seems to be the biggest reason I can't eat anything that hasn't been reared at home.

"I'm frustrated I don't know enough about cooking," Debbie complained that night in bed. Late at night in bed was where all our major conversations took place.

"You're kidding," I said, leaning up on an elbow.

"No. I know the basics and I can do stuff, but I'm running out of places to learn what I don't know."

"What don't you know?"

167

She looked at me. "I don't know."

"I'm confused," I said, lying back.

"So am I. I know that I need to know more, but what I need to know isn't what I'm learning. I need to know —" She sat up suddenly. "What if there was a war or something and we had to survive on our own without any shops or any outside help? What if you lost your job completely? What if we really had to be self-sufficient?"

"You've gone from Earth Mother to the mother in *The Terminator*. Do you want to start kick-boxing and weapons training?"

"I'm serious. We need to be more self-sufficient."

"I am not growing my hair!"

"You don't have to have long hair to be self-sufficient. Besides, you couldn't, you're going bald."

"I am not!"

She fussed my head with her hand. "Look, I just feel that we're missing out on things, but I don't know where to go, or where to look to find them. I feel really frustrated."

"Tense? Frustrated? Mmmm, well, you could always —" I snuggled up to her.

"Simon! Oh, I knew you wouldn't understand."

I sat up, too. "Okay, look, I thought we were doing really well. I haven't moaned for days."

"You moaned at lunchtime. You moaned that you smelt of pigs."

"You were the one who said I smelt of pigs. Pongo pig, you called me."

168

"Yes, well. I think I'm going to speak to the butcher in the village, see if he'll let me work in his shop for nothing so I can learn, or better still, see if he'll give me some lessons!"

CHAPTER
TWENTY-ONE

Food was becoming very important, and I guess growing our own vegetables was the next step, maybe even a step we should have taken before now, but we just had no experience and no idea where to start. If I'm honest, I also lacked inclination. Standing in a mud patch picking out weeds and talking to cabbages wasn't high on my "to do" list. Working full-time, I could afford to nip out to the local greengrocer's and spend a bit on vegetables for the week. Working part-time, the difference in income meant I didn't have that luxury anymore. We had to look at growing things ourselves.

We negotiated a spot with our landlady next to her vegetable garden, and I started weeding and clearing a large section ready to plant. It's hard work. Backbreaking work. The thought of spending days bent over a spade and fork churning over the ground was more than I could bear. Instead, I ran some temporary fence posts around the outside of the vegetable garden, put some wire round it, attached a small pulsar and battery and hooked out a couple of 10-week-old piglets to put in there and do the work for us.

"This could become a thriving business," I told Debbie, while we sipped ice-cold wine and watched the weaners root around eating all the weeds and grass, and slurping on the slugs and snails, fertilising as they went. What more could you ask for?

"Rent a Couple of Pigs to Clear Your Garden, dot, co, dot, north Devon," she said.

"Why not? As long as it's within our holding area, it would be legal. The pigs get fed for free, and everyone's veg patch gets cleared ready for planting. Win-win situation."

"Until the pigs escape."

"Well, yeah, there is that."

"It would probably be tricky on the insurance, too."

"Possibly."

"And I'm not sure how much you could charge. I'm not sure they'd qualify for an hourly minimum wage."

"You're right, it's a crap idea. Shame, though."

It was a shame, because it worked beautifully. Within 10 days, I took the pigs off and we were ready to plant. Only, it's not that easy. I've never had a garden, and I just assumed that you dig a hole, sprinkle in some seeds, cover it with manure — we have lots of manure — and come back in two months' time ready to feast on the produce.

After planting the seeds and growing nothing but some healthy and happy weeds, without a hint of anything edible among them, I went calling on the neighbours, all of whom had vibrant veg patches crammed with lots of healthy-looking vegetables, and asked if they had any ideas where I'd gone wrong.

They knew exactly where I'd gone wrong. They'd been watching my efforts with amused interest. They said they'd like to have come over and put me right, but they were having way too much fun for that.

I'd made a few mistakes. Actually, I'd made about all the mistakes it's possible to make. So I started again. It was late in the season, but I was assured I'd at least get something from it if I followed their instructions. First off, I was an arse if I thought that on Exmoor, where it was wet and cold nearly all the time, a seed would simply grow out of the ground. Plants are started off in little trainers, inside the house on a warm windowsill if we didn't have a greenhouse (which we didn't), where they can be mollycoddled until they're tough enough to go outside. So that's what we did, and they were right: it worked.

Meanwhile, Debbie went off to speak to the butcher who was delighted someone was that keen and wanted to learn, and between them they arranged a series of lessons.

"Wine?" Debbie asked, after she'd spent a long day in the butcher's shop learning everything there was to learn about offal.

"Mm, cheers," I replied, lifting my glass. We were in the vegetable garden, so called because it contained vegetables. Yes, we were finally a veg-growing family. We were independent in vegetables. Self-sufficient in greens. We would walk through supermarkets right past the vegetable aisles calling loudly, "We don't need this aisle, we grow our own!"

"No, I don't mean do you want more wine, I mean I want to start making our own wine next."

172

The most frightening thing about that sentence was the word "next". Next implied there was more to come. Next implied there was a list we were working our way through. How come nobody had told me about this list?

"What do you mean, next?" I said.

"Why do you always go off on tangents? It's so infuriating. Why can't you just talk normally? I just meant next because we're doing stuff. Making wine is what I'd like to do next, after the thing we did last. I'd just like to make some wine."

So there is a list! I wonder how I can get a copy?

"What type of wine?"

"Peapod wine? Dandelion wine?"

"You're making that up! There's no such thing as dandelion wine."

"Of course there is. It's supposed to be very nice. You can make wine out of anything apparently," she said.

"Yeah, but none of it is drinkable. I'll stick to chardonnay, thanks very much."

Looking hurt, she said, "You wouldn't drink any if I made it?"

How do you answer that? "I guess we could give it a go," I said.

The clue to how it tasted lies in the fact that it was ready in eight weeks. Imagine pouring a glass of ice-cold nail varnish remover, dipping a dandelion into it and giving it a swirl before taking a sip.

"Oh my God, it's making the back of my eyeballs itch — is it supposed to do that?" I stammered. "Is it even safe? My goodness, there are drug cartels in

Afghanistan that would be all over this recipe: 'Forget the poppies, lads, we're moving into dandelions'"

"It's not *that* bad," she said, braving a second sip. "It's maybe a little young."

"Young! It's still a foetus. If it were any younger, the dandelions would still be in the ground. Sorry, sweetheart, and I know I'm not the first to say this, but life's too short to drink bad wine."

"Well, I think it's drinkable," she said.

"Just go steady with it, okay?" I was genuinely worried for her. Then again, if she did get hammered, there was a chance she might let me into her secret list, so although I tried to look after her, I didn't try to stop her.

It didn't make any difference. Just when her lips became nicely lubricated so she could get them around some of her inner thoughts, thoughts that I hoped would include the list, she fell asleep. However, it didn't put her off home brewing or fermenting, and with a little practice we started making some acceptable drinks: chilli vodka and sloe gin, then sloe cider and blackcurrant cordial, elderflower cordial and, the best, elderflower champagne. But the wine was always iffy.

I continued going back to work in London every other week, worked hard and didn't trash another restaurant. When I was home, Debbie and I continued to throw our hearts into working the land, the animals and the lifestyle.

I rode out most days and went back to riding Georgie much more than Bobby simply because Georgie was more supple, faster and I could do more

174

with her — a little dressage, a little showjumping, that sort of thing. But on the ground, Bobby and I were brother-and-sister close.

After riding and sorting out Georgie, I'd move over to Bobby and open up, telling her everything that was going on while I groomed her and fussed over her. I'd have breakfast, and then Debbie and I would go down to work on the land. Lack of money meant we were doing everything ourselves, flying solo on tasks that we had no right to be flying solo on. Debbie was good with ideas, while I was a botcher, making things up as I went along. In other words, a liability. Yet when it came to the animals, I didn't cut corners, which is why when the sheep needed shearing, I booked myself onto a shearing course at an agricultural college.

I went along, and someone who looked very much like he'd drunk dandelion wine for breakfast his entire life taught me how to separate a sheep from its wool with the least amount of blood spilt — mine or the sheep's.

Then I came home to do mine.

Be afraid, little sheepies, be very afraid.

The hardest thing was catching one. Clearly, none of them wanted to go first. I finally got hold of one, plonked her on her bum, switched on the clippers and set about running them tight between her skin and her woolly coat.

Things went well for a while. Fleece was tumbling away from her, revealing pinky white skin beneath, and I was doing all the right footfalls and twists that I'd learned at college. She just sat there, while I moved

175

around her removing hunks of wool. The problem came when I was about halfway through.

For a start, my sheep are an awful lot fatter than the ones I had been practising on, so I had about twice as much to shear, going up and down over rolls of fat. They're also a traditional breed with really long wool. In short, I got halfway through shearing and got lost. Well, I didn't get lost, the sheep got lost. I knew she was in there somewhere, I just couldn't find her beneath all the cut fleece. I had to stop, call her name and wait until she answered before I could locate her head and carry on.

To shear 20 sheep took me three days. Professional shearers are paid 50 pence a sheep. Two days at college, three days shearing, I saved a tenner. Well done me.

In addition to saving money, we had to try and figure out a way of buying things cheaply or getting them without any money changing hands at all. The best currency we found was eggs.

The current exchange rate is a pound for half a dozen free-range eggs, and yes, you can go into a shop (as long as you know the owner), buy goods and pay with eggs. On several occasions I've even bought petrol with them. It's bartering, swapping our goods for theirs. The eggs were flying, and we decided we needed more chickens, but we couldn't afford to buy them. So we decided to hatch our own.

We got hold of an old incubator and started hatching little baby chicks, which, while easier and a lot less messy than Debbie's boobs, wasn't nearly as much fun. In a year, the flock increased to 40 laying chickens and

60 meat birds. I missed Red because I think he would've had a wonderful time with all those ladies. White enjoyed himself and did what needed doing, he just didn't do it with quite as much panache or energy as Red would've done. At the end of a long, hot summer's day, White looked wiped out, whereas Red would've been doing "come here" movements with his wings, saying, "Bring me more vomen." For some reason, I always think of him speaking with an Italian accent.

CHAPTER
TWENTY-TWO

We were talking one evening about the chickens and the pigs when Debbie said, "That First-Time Mum needs to come up into the maternity ward." The maternity ward was the name we had given to a small brick shed in the top field opposite the house.

The First-Time Mum was a young, pretty pig that was having the General's babies for the first time. She was a lovely little lady with an obvious bump, and very confident and happy with it, but all first-time mothers need a little extra help. The next day I strawed down the maternity ward and together we moved her in, 10 days before she was due. There we kept an eye on her.

On her due day, we hung around sneaking little looks to see if anything was happening. Pigs give lots of warning before they give birth. Most obviously they build a huge nest with a neat furrow down the centre, in which they lie before they go into labour. She built the nest, and the contractions started.

"I'm going in to see," I whispered, feeling the familiar tingle of excitement.

I sneaked in. "It's okay, pretty girl, it's only me," I said softly, making my way around her to the busy end. I told her she was clever, and I told her it was okay, everything would be fine, and I sat there for ages. Nothing happened. She was in labour, she was pushing and having contractions, but nobody was coming out.

I felt inside her. I could feel a nose, but the gap it was trying to pass though was too small. I tried to stretch her, gently making the gap bigger by running my finger around and around it, but it wasn't just a little bit too small, it was massively too small. This was out of my league.

Debbie rushed off to call the vet, and he arrived within the hour.

"The piglet inside her is a whopper," he said, giving her an injection to increase the contractions and squeezing bottle after bottle of lubricant into her through a tube. "Hopefully, this will work, but it doesn't look good. Her baby is just too big and he's stuck."

"Is he still alive?" I asked.

He shook his head. "No, he would have died a while ago. I would think all the others still inside her are, too. That's the problem. They're going to start rotting soon. Give her tonight and see if she can deliver them. I'll phone in the morning."

Debbie and I took turns lying next to her in the straw and stayed with her all through the night. She tried so hard. She knew it wasn't right, knew something was wrong, and I could hear her panting and pushing in the dark, and I held her trotter, stroked her leg and prayed to God like I've never prayed to God before to help her.

I kept thinking she'd done it. I kept hearing squelchy noises and flicked the torch on hoping to find the piglet out. But it never was.

In the morning, she was exhausted. She didn't have any strength left. The vet phoned and I told him there was no change. He said it had gone on long enough. He was sorry. She needed to be put out of her misery. I said I'd sort it.

Oh dear God.

It was early in the morning. I had to go to London to work. I couldn't *not* go. I hugged Debbie for ages, knowing what I was leaving her to. Then I climbed into my car and drove away.

She phoned several hours later. I was still on the road. I pulled over.

She was sobbing. She had called a professional, and he had come down and shot the First-Time Mother. Her contractions had stopped. She was just too tired. Bless her . . .

. . . bless her little heart.

Then he winched her away.

She said she could still hear the shot ringing in her ears.

"Oh Simon . . . Oh Simon . . ." she sobbed. I didn't hear anything else, because I was sobbing, too.

CHAPTER
TWENTY-THREE

I drove to my mother's, figuring I'd spend the night in my room, but when I parked up and walked in, she had company. Ziggy. Debbie had called him, explained what happened with the First-Time Mother and asked him to come round and take me out. The last thing in the world I wanted was to go out, so I told him to bugger off — it's only Ziggy after all.

I called Debbie. She answered on the third ring with a question. "Is Ziggy there, is he with you?"

"He is," I said, looking across at Ziggy, who had my mother dashing about after him in a way that she never did with me. "I don't want to go out, though. I just want to be depressed tonight. I don't want to act like it doesn't matter or it didn't happen. I feel really bad, really, really bad. Poor First-Time Mother."

"I knew you'd say that, but I really think you should go out. It's not healthy for you to sit alone and brood on today."

"But it's okay for you to do it?"

"I'm not," she said, "I've got Paula here."

Paula is everything Ziggy isn't: sensible, loyal, trustworthy, clever and sober. Paula wouldn't abandon you in a club if she got lucky. I felt I had the raw end of the friend deal.

Again I told Ziggy that I didn't want to go. I told him I wanted to lie on my bed and read. Really, no, I don't want to go. So he said okay and went upstairs ahead of me. When I walked into my room, he was already lying on one side of the bed. "I'll stay with you," he said, patting a spot next to him. "What shall we read?"

"You're right," I said. "Let's go out."

We went to a packed loud bar, and he introduced me to a crowd and began telling them all about me.

"Tell them how much you paid for a full tank of petrol to get down here," he insisted.

I tried to send him a no with a tiny shake of my head, but it didn't work. In the end, I told them: "Twenty pounds, two dozen eggs, a joint of pork and two pork chops." It made me feel like a Martian being asked about his cute ship. Tonight of all nights, I wanted to feel as though I was one of them, a Londoner, not a freak outsider. Couldn't they see that?

It was all a mistake. I shouldn't have gone. Three beers in and I told the story of the First-Time Mother, her babies dying and rotting inside of her, and having her shot while she was still in labour. I don't think I'll be invited out with them again.

Ziggy got lucky with a girl in a long flowing skirt and an expensive hairstyle who smelled like an Estee Lauder aisle. I wondered if I smelt of pigs. If I did, nobody said anything.

I walked home alone. The next morning I phoned Debbie first thing. She was still in bed and said she didn't want to get up for a month.

"Are you okay?" I asked.

"Yes. I'm sad about yesterday, and I'm a bit worried about everything else."

"What do you mean everything else?"

"Money. The animals. Everything. We can't afford to do any shopping this week — we can only just afford to feed the animals. The electricity people are threatening to cut us off, we're behind on the rent, the car is so illegal it's untrue; the MOT's run out and so has the tax and there's simply no money to get them done. We're going to have a vet bill in for yesterday, and one from the bodyman who took the First-Time Mother away. I just don't know what we're going to do."

"Blimey," I said.

"Blimey's right. At this rate you're going to get your wish and we will be going back to live in London."

"I'm not sure I can go back now," I admitted. "And besides, the animals are my best friends. I couldn't leave Bobby, or Dex, or Kylie, or the General, or any of them. I'll ask for more work, see if I can earn some extra money."

Over coffee and toast, while getting ready for work, I asked my mum for more work. The thing is, I couldn't tell my mother how broke we really were — estate agents are very serious around money: the level of anybody's success is measured by the wad in their wallet and little else. So I told her what I thought I

183

could get away with. She didn't take the hint. Neither did she offer me any more work.

"We could do a farmers' market and sell some of our pork," Debbie said.

"Of course!"

For the rest of the week we both got busy. Debbie worked out the logistics and legalities of selling pork to the public, what we needed to do, who we needed to contact, insurance, an approved packing station (we hired the local butcher's shop in which she'd been taking lessons), how to label the meat, registering with environmental health, sourcing bags, aprons and hats, a table cloth and a portable chiller cabinet to sell from, designing leaflets and business cards and finding us a local pitch in a farmers' market. I on the other hand decided I'd make us a fortune as a writer. Good plan! I spent the week drafting a catchy letter to all the Devon magazine editors telling them I was available for commissions.

Incredibly, the editor of the biggest-selling Devon magazine, *Devon Life*, phoned me the next day. She phoned me. Me. Phoned. The next day.

"I can't commission you, but let's see what you can do. Write me something original about your part of North Devon and send it to me with lots of lovely photographs," she said. "Then we'll see."

I was going to be famous and rich beyond our wildest dreams.

"We pay 45 pounds if it's published."

Maybe not that rich.

When I got home, I jumped on Georgie and rode out onto the moor for the day. We went all around Hoar Oak and up to Brendon Two Gates, and when I got back, I wrote about it. Then I sent it in. I didn't even get an acknowledgement. So much for becoming a writer.

The farmers' market approach was more successful.

"We're booked in for next Saturday," Debbie told me. That Friday evening, we sat outside the butcher's shop, waiting for him to close. When the last customer left, clutching a small bag of meat, the owner switched the sign on the door to "Closed", and in we went.

He gave us the keys, told us how to lock up and left.

"What now?" I said as he shut the door behind him and whistled his way up the road.

"Now we butcher and pack," Debbie said, opening the door to the cold store so the freezing air blasted into my face. Hanging inside was one of our pigs cut in two halves. I brought out one half and we started.

It's okay butchering a pig. There are a couple of tricky cuts, but it's not too difficult. However, it is heavy and physical, which I guess is why butchers don't bother stopping off at the gym on the way home from work. We had the radio on and we chatted while we cut, chopped and sawed through bones, minced, made sausages and mixed black pudding. When it was all in recognisable bits, we packed and wrapped, weighed and labelled. It was nearly midnight when we finished. We stacked it carefully in boxes, slipped it back into the cold store and went home.

CHAPTER
TWENTY-FOUR

On the morning of the farmers' market, we left home before dawn and made our way down onto the land, shining torches into the blinking eyes of the animals to wake them up with an early breakfast. That time of day has a certain smell, different from any other: it's earthy, kind of heavy, like walking off an aeroplane in a cold country. The weight of the outside world made me feel even more tired.

None of the animals were hungry. Who could blame them, they weren't even awake! Bobby couldn't eat for yawning, which made me yawn, which made her yawn, which made me . . . I had to turn around and leave before we slumped down together for a nap.

When the animals were done, I drove to the cold store and Debbie helped me load the car. Then we set off for the market 20 miles away in South Molton.

The trouble is, how can you make raw meat look attractive? We set it all out and then fiddled. We piled the sausages high, laid the chops in neat rows and set the joints best side up. When it was done, we stood there and watched the punters stroll by without a glance in our direction.

"It's you," Debbie said. "You look moody. You're putting people off."

"Gee, thanks. Anyway, I'm not moody, I'm tired."

"Well, act like you're happy."

"I am happy. Happy and tired."

"Can't you smile or something? You can be tired and smile at the same time, can't you?"

I smiled. It didn't help. Halfway through the day we'd only sold one chop. Then Debbie cuddled up to me, nuzzled my neck and whispered something stupid that made me laugh, and someone walked up to the stall.

Debbie elbowed me out of the way and pounced on them, telling them about the pigs that were happy and running in the woods. The person loved it and spent a fortune. For the rest of the day we did the kissy, kissy couple thing, which was fine by me, and laughed and joked. People came up to us and we had queues and everything. We told stories about the pigs that made people laugh and they all bought something.

"We sold out, sold out, sold out," Debbie sang in the car. We stopped on the way home at a feed store and bought animal food and extra tasty treats for the pigs as a thank you.

"If we can do that every week, with your wages on top, we can at least survive," Debbie said.

We could, but we had a lot of mouths to feed:

Two horses, Georgie and Bobby

One Kylie pig

Four breeding sows

Piglets of various ages

The General Lee, a super-cool boar
Dex, my gorgeous, one-eyed puppy
Darcy, the mummy's boy Great Dane
Sheep
Lucky-Turkey-Leaky
Geese
Ducks
Chickens
White, the cockerel

After we'd done the rounds that evening of feeding, watering and bedding down, Debbie said, "I need to go out tonight. I don't care if we sit in a pub behind one drink each and then leave. I *really* need to go out. We haven't been out for months. I need to wear a nice dress. I need to do my hair. I need to put on makeup. I need to put something on my feet other than welly boots. If you mention McDonalds, I will behead you with a karate chop."

"You can't do karate," I said.

"Well, you can't eat McDonalds."

"No, but it doesn't stop me wanting to eat it. The thought of a Big Mac . . ."

"You couldn't do it."

"I know. You've ruined me."

"Aahhhh, poor thing," she cuddled up to me, kissing me on the cheek and whispering in my ear, "You've pulled. You can take me out tonight."

We went to the Blue Ball Inn at the top of Countisbury hill. If you close your eyes and imagine a country inn with logs crackling in the heart of an inglenook fireplace, low ceilings, old-fashioned candles that actually run with wax and over-stuffed sofas to sink into, that's where we were. We made our way to the bar and ordered two drinks.

"Are you the pig people?" the barman asked, filling two large glasses with wine.

I tried to sniff myself. I thought I smelt of shower gel, but I couldn't be certain there wasn't an undercurrent of odour oinker.

We said we were. He nodded, "Thought so. I was going to try and get in contact with you. Would you like our beer slops for your pigs? We're just tipping it away at the moment, and it seems such a waste."

"Are you kidding? We'd love them!" I said.

"Come by tomorrow around lunchtime when it's quieter. You'll need some containers, there's about 50 litres. You can have that every week."

Fifty litres of beer a week!

Excuse me while I do a little jig of joy . . .

"I'm going to have a pint with the General," I said when we'd found a seat by the fire. "Two men of the world propping up the side of the pig arc putting the world to rights."

"Ooh, can I come down and play, too?" she said, over-doing the sarcasm somewhat.

"Sorry, no. It's men's hour. Girls not allowed. Anyway, the conversation will be way above your pretty little maid's head."

She flicked up her eyebrows and tutted.

"We will intellectualise the football transfer window; philosophise on the LBW rule; debate the off-side trap; and generally —"

"Talk a load of old toot," she cut in.

"Yeah, talk a load of old toot," I smiled and touched her leg. "Of course you can come down and play; you can help us with our studies of what makes women tick." The pub was packed, the sounds of laughter the main noise. There were some locals, but it was predominantly holidaymakers — you could tell that from the lack of colourful farmer's string used to accessorise muddy jeans or wellies.

"Fifty litres," Debbie mused. "Fantastic for fattening. I wonder if we'll be able to taste it in the meat? Won't they get drunk?"

"I shouldn't think so. Their body mass is too huge to worry about a drop of beer. Besides, I'll be spreading it out between all of them."

I was wrong. They did get drunk. Horrendously drunk.

The next evening I fed all of them nuts as usual, then filled a bucket with beer for each of the pens. The beer smelled glorious — hoppy and creamy, and it was as dark as oak. There was even a head on the top.

I carried the first bucket in to the General. It's a big moment when a man has his first beer with his best friend. It shows the level the friendship has reached and takes it onto a new plane. I went over and punched the General in a matey way on the shoulder. "My round," I said and put down the bucket in front of him, careful not to slosh any of the contents over the side.

He sniffed it and took a sip.

190

"So, did you see the game last night?" I said, figuring there's always a game on somewhere, even if I hadn't watched one in years. "Unbelievable, wasn't it! How's your beer?"

He blew bubbles into the bucket and sneezed before wandering back over to his dinner without a second glance, or having any more than that first sip. How disappointing. I really thought we could bond over a pint.

"Look out, misses coming through!" I called. Behind him, his Wife of Right Now spotted the bucket and came harrowing over, put her head in the bucket and downed the lot. She drank loudly, snorting, sucking and slurping, and when she finally lifted her head, with frothy liquid dribbling down her chin, smacked her lips, shook, burped and went back to her meal, the bucket was empty.

I put the beer in each of the other pens, but saved a drop for one more try with the General. I took it in, and then I saw Wife of Right Now. The alcohol had hit. She was propped up on an elbow, one eye shut so she could focus better through the other. She hiccupped, nosed about for a bite of dinner, missed, wobbled and slumped over onto her side.

Whoops. I looked at the other pens. Piglets were quarrelling everywhere, doing the bite-bite motion with their mouths and telling each other to sod off. The sows were moving about with a bouncer's swagger, looking like they wanted nothing better than to duff someone up, if only they could catch them without running because going anywhere in a straight line slowly was a bit of an issue, let alone speeding up.

I watched in horror. There were running races, tugs of war, scraps and, the worst, wrestling . . .

"Ladies and gentlemen, it's time for the wrestling! In the dirt corner, unbeaten in no previous contests and really stroppy tonight after a good long glug of beer, I give you, Sulky Teenage Boy Piglet!

"In the other corner by the tree, again untested but looking mean and moody tonight, I give you, Teenage Girl Piglet!

"Three falls or a submission. Shake hands and come out wrestling.

"Let the tournament . . . begin!"

It was horrific. Two piglets launched themselves at each other. They kicked up dust as they span, ducked and dived, trying to trip the other up so they fell and could be jumped on. The others crowded around, not quite chanting "Fight, fight, fight", but not far from it. Then in the middle of the bout for no apparent reason, they turned away from each other and dashed off in different directions. End of tournament, thank goodness.

Imagine a classroom full of children, all given sugary drinks, chocolate and sweets with loads of additives, and then let loose in a gym. That's what it was like. It was a massive rush of energy and adrenalin, but it was short lived. Soon, they began to pucker out, calming down, flopping out, snoozing and sleeping wherever they found themselves. The adults, however, had far more staying power.

Wife of Right Now in with the General got to her feet, made her way over to her house and took a chunk out of the wall.

"Hey!" I yelled, rushing in. "Cut it out, will you! There's no need to beat the house up."

But there was. There was a massive need to beat the house up, and all of the sows felt it. Taking their lead from Wife of Right Now, the sows ripped into their houses, smashing the sides out, yanking down the roofs, biting into the struts, tearing up the floors, simply decimating their place.

"You destructive . . . pigs!" I screamed. "Vandals! Hooligans! You should be ashamed of yourselves!" I sank down about as low as the houses now stood and watched the sows finish their demolition job.

The next morning I was still fuming. I wanted to punish them, punish them all. I wanted to make them suffer. I made the biggest, greasiest double-egg sandwich you've ever seen, smothered it in ketchup, carefully wrapped it in foil to keep it fresh and warm and went down to the pigs and their destroyed pens and houses. The pigs were everywhere, sprawled out asleep in the dirt where they'd fallen (except the General, who's a good boy). I unwrapped the egg sandwich and went around wafting it under their nose and taking out a bite of it in front of every pig. They groaned.

Later that day I phoned the pub and said we probably wouldn't collect any more beer. Then I set about rebuilding the houses. It took me weeks, especially as the pigs, now sober, decided they wanted

193

to help. They kept moving things. I put down the hammer, and they thought it would be much better in the dirt over there rather than right next to me within handy grabbing distance. It would have been okay if it took me twice as long, but it didn't: it took much longer than that.

CHAPTER
TWENTY-FIVE

The houses hadn't been long completed when I was taking a morning off, sitting at the computer checking emails. Debbie was off doing the morning animal rounds when she came roaring back on the quad bike. I watched her out the window. She staggered off the bike. She was all over the place, rushing, but not getting anywhere fast.

I ran out. She couldn't talk. She took a deep breath, calmed down and said, "Bobby's down. You go to her, I'll phone the vet."

I zoomed off feeling so scared. I'm not sure how old she is, but for a big horse she's well into pensionable age. I'd hardly ridden her for the past year and a half. I just fussed her, changed her rugs and made her look beautiful, which wasn't hard.

I knew which field she was in and cut the engine to the bike just far enough away so she wouldn't be disturbed, got off and ran the rest of the way to the gate. I could see her a little way in. She was on her side. I opened the gate and made myself walk.

When I reached her, I crouched down, stroking her neck gently. I didn't want to frighten her, so I forced my voice to go light. "Hey, pretty girl, are you having a lie-in this morning, sweetheart?"

She looked up. There was blood around her nose. "Aw, my pretty girl, it's okay. It's all okay." Tears pricked my eyes, but I tried not to let it come through in my voice.

She tried to get up, tried to get up for me. "No, no, no, no. You stay there." She stopped trying and rested her chin on the grass. We looked at each other. Her beautiful big eyes. I desperately didn't want to cry, desperately didn't want to worry, or upset, or frighten her, but I couldn't help it. Tears washed down my cheeks, my nose ran, and I backhanded it all away and tried to laugh to cover it.

"You're so beautiful, nothing's going to happen to you. I'll look after you, I promise."

She watched me. She just . . . watched me. I stroked her, I smiled, and I told her how much I loved her, told her over and over and over again.

The vet arrived and did his tests. He was thorough, and kind. But there was nothing he could do. She was old. She was ready. It was her time.

I nodded. I bit down with my teeth and dug my thumb nails into the tips of my fingers. All I could manage was a one-word question, a question that was so loaded it could have been nuclear. "Nothing?"

"No, I'm sorry. The kindest thing . . ."

He did the kindest thing. I held her and whispered I loved her, while she slipped away. I started covering her head with a rug when Debbie, tears in her eyes too, stopped me.

196

"Let me bring Georgie over. She needs to know Bobbie's gone so she won't keep looking out for her." She brought Georgie over. Georgie approached Bobbie's body slowly. She bent down her head and sniffed her, then threw her head right back and let out the loudest squeal. With that, Debbie led her away.

I covered Bobbie's head and her bum so the crows couldn't get to her, and walked away.

She was fine the previous night, she ate her dinner, and we had fusses. Debbie said she was fine this morning and ate her breakfast. There'd been no sign of anything wrong. She just ran out of life. It was just her time. That's the logical side that I try — I try so hard — to cling to and concentrate on, because the other thoughts just make me want to curl up and die.

By rights, the vet said, she should have keeled over and died on the spot. She didn't. She waited for me, and that breaks my heart. I've never had my heart broken before, not properly, not like this. It hurts so much. It really, really hurts so much. I miss you so much, my baby girl.

CHAPTER
TWENTY-SIX

"I've sorted out a companion for Georgie," Debbie announced later in the day. The thing is you can't keep a horse on its own. They need company. Georgie needed a new friend, and she needed one today.

I looked up. "You have? Who?"

"Pandora!"

I groaned. Pandora. Of course it was going to be Pandora. "Pandora," I said.

"Yep, Pandora."

"Steph's Pandora?"

She nodded.

"Old, cantankerous, belligerent, stroppy, hates people; hates other horses; hates everything really; and definitely hates men."

"That's the one!"

"Great."

We introduced Georgie and Pandy, and they flew at each other like warring sisters. But within a few days it calmed down to your normal, average, can't-stand-one-another female feud. Which was much better.

I tried to keep busy. I got up and I did stuff all day long. Then I went to bed. I tried to do things that were kind of Bobby related, telling myself that I was doing them for her, like planting a tree for her or cutting back the stinging nettles in her field so it looked cared for, and then I struck a superb idea. I'd muck spread all her droppings onto the field: that way, she'd be giving life to the grass. It seemed like a nice thing to do.

I shovelled every last scrap into a trailer fixed to the back of the quad bike and drove into the centre of the field. I got a fork, opened the back, dug into a huge chunk, weighed it and then flung it so it sprayed off to one side. I did it again and again. Flinging it to the left was easy, but that's all I was doing. I needed some on the right. I attempted the, some might say — and please don't try this at home unless you're a professional or have someone with extensive medical training standing by with an air ambulance warmed up, rotors turning — ultra difficult "over the head and flicked off to the right" fling.

It didn't fling. The Bobby poo went up in the air and came down on my head. Bits of it even slithered down the inside of my glasses. I sat down on the edge of the trailer and started laughing. I looked up. "You bitch," I shouted. I imagined Bobby looking down, snorting, shaking her head, her mane flicking back and forth.

I went up to the house for a bath.

"You stink!" Debbie said, "What have you been doing?"

"Muck spreading. It went a bit wrong. I need a kiss."

"No chance!"

"Yes chance!" I started chasing her around the house. She was shrieking and laughing and so was I. It was a good moment.

"You're in a better mood," she said.

I smiled.

"Good, because you've got some post."

"Bills?" I said, with a knot forming in my stomach. Money was still frighteningly tight.

"I don't think so. It's a big A4 envelope."

I picked it up and opened it. Inside were just two sheets, two pages cut out from a magazine. I slipped them out and looked at them. It was my article. The article I'd written and sent in to the magazine. They'd published it.

In the space of a week I'd lost my best friend and become a published writer, one of the worst things and one of the best things ever to happen to me, which is difficult to deal with when they happen on top of each other. I didn't know whether to mope about or celebrate, so I ate chocolate, which kind of works for both.

Pandora was no substitute for Bobby. She hates me — why do all the women hate me on first sight? I felt like taking her down to Kylie and saying, "She used to hate me, too! You're not alone, but she doesn't hate me now — go on tell her . . . Tell her you don't hate me now . . ." I wonder if different species can understand one another, whether they can pick up the odd word and catch the gist? I would've given it a go, but horses hate pigs, and Pandora's natural hatred towards everything in the world would only compound that. Probably not a good idea to introduce them then.

So I worked on bringing Pandora around the old-fashioned way, which is to say I fussed around her and did everything for her, but ignored her at the same time, which, trust me, is a far faster way of getting a female to notice you in a good way than fawning all over her. Still it took months. I ignored her, and she hated me, and we got on with our own agendas.

"She'll come around," Debbie promised. "Just give her time."

How much time can you give a woman to come around?

"You're good with women," Debbie continued, not quite looking me in the eye.

Red alert slammed on inside my head. *Incoming! Abandon ship! Run for your lives!* "No, really, I'm not," I assured her.

"Yes, you are. You know you are. Anyway, I thought you might like the idea of getting a wild boar sow — how exciting would that be?"

A wild boar woman, that sounds friendly — *not!* "A wild boar! But they're dangerous, aren't they?"

"Well, some say they're to pigs what a wolf is to a dog. That can't be true of this one because her name is Miss Piggy."

"That's even worse," I exclaimed. "Ironic names are always bad, like calling someone Tiny when they're six foot eight, or Slim when they're 20 stone. Or Miss Piggy when they're a savage wild boar!"

"Don't be silly. The people who own her . . . their children named her. She's lovely, very friendly, and it would give us a real edge, something different to offer. Wild boar pork is so sought after."

"I'm not surprised. It's right up there in the danger stakes with rhino rump or alligator steaks. I have enough trouble with Pandora trying to kill me when the mood takes her, which is pretty much all the time. The thought of a wild boar at it, too — no, we are *not* getting a wild boar, and that's my final word on the matter."

CHAPTER
TWENTY-SEVEN

We got the wild boar. A proper wild boar, at least four-fifths wild boar; the other fifth we were assured was a touch of Tamworth, but four-fifths of wild killer beast is enough for me, even if she is called Miss Piggy.

We collected her and brought her onto the land. I backed the trailer with her inside into the woods and dropped the ramp, then ran.

"You silly arse," Debbie shouted in hysterics as I hurdled the electric fencing at full speed next to her, before slowing down and making my way back to her side. Behind me, nothing. Miss Piggy hadn't even emerged. We saw the trailer shudder, then all went quiet. I peeked in: she was lying down on her side, her head nestled in the straw, nodding off to sleep.

"All the pigs love the trailer," I said, gently tapping the metal side to encourage her out. "Come on, Miss Piggy — oh, look, I can't call her that. Can't we change her name?"

"What to?"

"Um," I thought about it. "She looks like a Geraldine, kind of distinguished, kind of scary, kind of bossy and not someone you want to mess with."

"And that's what Geraldines are?"

"Probably not all of them, but some are. Besides, I watched *The Vicar of Dibley* last night, and I think I've got a crush on Dawn French."

It took the entire afternoon for Geraldine to venture out and only then because I shook a bucket of feed at the end of the trailer.

"She hates me," I said.

"She does not hate you. She doesn't even know you."

"That's the problem. They all hate me before they know me." Life to any estate agent is cram-packed full of people who hate you without even knowing you, and some who do. That's the nature of the beast. I couldn't see the nature of this beast was going to be any different.

"Bobby didn't hate you on first sight. Neither did Black Bum or Spotty Bum. That was love at first sight."

"I didn't tell them I was an estate agent."

"Well, you're only a part-time estate agent now."

"I don't want to be a full-time farmer."

"No, I know you don't."

"I need to shave my head. Do you think I look scruffy?" I looked down and brushed my jeans with my hands. "No!" I squealed. "When did I start wearing jeans? I don't remember starting wearing jeans? I bet I look scruffy. I do, I look scruffy. I know I do. Do I look scruffy?"

She rolled her eyes.

When Geraldine was settled and comfortable in her new home and didn't look as if she was going to escape and savage everyone in the county, we took a sneaky day off.

It was a beautiful hot summer's day. We did the animals together early in the morning and then took off for Putsborough beach, just outside Croyde — the surf capital of Devon. We walked hand in hand along the sand in bare feet, past all the girls who'd taken a sicky from work or bunked off school and sat there with their skirts pulled up just high enough to tan their legs, as well as families with young children dashing about and digging holes with bright plastic toy shovels.

"This is the life," I said, turning my face up to the sun and feeling the rays penetrate all the way down to my bones.

"Mm. Why don't you take your top off?" Debbie said.

"I can't."

"Why ever not?"

"Because I'd rather not."

"But you're hot."

All right. I did.

She stopped and whistled.

"It looks like you've been beaten up by a herd of wild Geraldines," she said. "Where did all the bruises, cuts, scrapes and . . ." she peered closer, ". . . bites happen?"

I shrugged. "You know."

"No, I don't. How did that one happen?" she said, pointing at a purple, yellow smudge on my upper arm.

"Well . . . that was a tree actually."

"A tree. Okay. And that one?"

"Pigs."

"Uh-uh. That one? Is that a bite?"

"Pandora."

"Mm. That one?"

"Sheep."

"Sheep?"

"Sheep."

"That one on your chest — is that a footprint?"

"Don't ask."

"Okay. That one?"

"That's enough," I said, pulling my top back on.

"It's not, I'm not even halfway through yet. What on earth do you do?"

"It's not me!" I complained.

"Is this why you wear a T-shirt to bed?"

No, I wear a T-shirt to bed because in the country it's freezing at night, unlike London where it's warm and houses are snuggled up close to one another, and people don't have to wear T-shirts to bed to stop the ice from settling on their skin.

Lovely, lovely warm London . . .

CHAPTER
TWENTY-EIGHT

Early winter. The tips of my ears are burning red, but that's the only part of me that is burning anything. The rest is just freezing. The memory of walking hand in hand along Putsborough beach with Debbie checking out my war wounds is just that, a memory. Summer's gone and we've decided not to bother with autumn this year and hurtled straight into winter.

I'm down doing the pigs when my mobile leaps into life. Damn. I shuffle faster with a water bucket in one hand, slopping freezing cold water into my welly boot, and a bucket of feed in the other hand.

There is nothing more maddening than a ringing phone you can't answer. It's not just the fact that you might miss an important call: it's the message that not picking up sends to the person ringing. It's a mobile. You can always answer a mobile.

"Coming through," I called, bumping heads with the bottom of the buckets on piglets that refused to budge out of my way. On the whole, the pigs are pretty contented and laze about most of the day, but at feed time, they turn into Tasmanian Devils. And the worst is Kylie.

In the winter, I use feed troughs because the ground is sludgy and it's not fair to feed them on the ground. Ahead I could see the troughs under the trees. The ringtone on my phone was reaching a crescendo, the piglets were screeching and woofing as they splashed through mud and puddles around me, and there, right in front like a solid black wall between me and the troughs, stood Kylie. The piglets are her little darlings, and most of the time she loves them. But when it comes to dinnertime, it was every pig for themselves, and she was older, wiser and hungrier than the rest, bless her little trotters.

With the piglets scooting around my feet, all I could do was pigeon-step forward, but as my little group drew closer to Kylie, I watched her hook a nose under the belly of a passing piglet and toss it, spinning it hip high through the air towards me. Great. Now I was under fire, too.

This was our nightly routine. Sometimes it made me laugh, sometimes I'd gasp when a piglet landed in a rough, tangled heap, but always I'd feel like the hero in a war movie, dashing across the battlefield bearing urgent supplies. Sometimes I made it intact, sometimes I'd be sent sprawling, the feed spilling with a bundle of pigs diving on top, and on a few memorable occasions when I fell over the food, pigs diving on top of me.

Tonight was different. Tonight I had a new determination. My phone was ringing. I held the buckets a little higher and pushed on.

208

Undeterred, Kylie shot another piglet at me. "Kylie, you're their mum," I yelled, sidestepping left. "Be nice to them."

I put down the water bucket. Delighted piglets scrambled towards it, only to sniff, turn up their noses and come charging back. It bought me a few moments, long enough to reach Kylie, who wasn't so easily tricked.

I threw some nuts over her shoulder and heard them clatter somewhere around the troughs. Kylie turned tail and trotted towards the sound of food. So we all — Kylie, piglets and me — reached the troughs at the same time.

I poured the feed in as long a line as I could, dived a hand into my pocket and pressed green without looking at the display.

A voice said, "Simon, it's mum, are you busy?"

I stepped back from the line of chomping pigs, in the mud, under the trees, in the pigpen, cold, with one welly boot full of icy water and threatening frostbite on my foot, and an empty bucket swinging in my hand. At least I was still upright. "Not at all."

She told me the housing market was in a bad way. She told me the office was struggling. She said she had too many staff. She didn't need them all. Someone had to go, so, byeeeeee. She probably said it a lot nicer than that, but that's the gist. I was out. *Oh no, I was out!*

I walked out of the pigpen unsure if I wanted to throw my phone in the river or myself. I didn't want to do a tally, but my mind did one anyway:

Two horses, Georgie and Pandora (I miss Bobby so much)

One Kylie pig

Four breeding sows

Geraldine, the wild boar

Piglets of various ages

The General Lee, the man of the farm

The dogs, Dex and Darcy

Ewes, hoggets and lambs

Lucky-Turkey-Leaky

Geese

Ducks

Chickens

White, the cockerel

That's it, my last tie with London is severed. I am unemployed. Trashed. Scrapped. Dumped, with about 120 hungry mouths to feed. This is the end. We can't bounce back from this. It's impossible. Bye-bye smallholding. Bye-bye Exmoor. Bye-bye self-sufficiency dream. I've been sacked from being an estate agent! Who is ever sacked from being an estate agent? Am I not even popular enough to hold a position in the most unpopular career that exists in the western hemisphere? It's like telling a slug he's sacked from being a slug. I liked being a slug. I liked being a London slug. What am I going to do now?

I finished feeding everyone, and then I crawled into Kylie's house, made my way to the back and curled up. I just wanted to hide. It was a long while before Kylie came in. When she did, she sniffed me before lying down. I made my way over to her, spooning up behind her. She smelled a bit piggy, but mostly all I could smell was the straw bed. I put my arm over her. It was comforting. I told her all about the phone call. It was kind of a practice for what would come later.

Later came soon after when I told the same story to Debbie. I'm not sure what I expected, certainly tears, anger, frustration, but she just got up, found some paper and a pen and settled down to making lists, trying to find a way of making things work. It reminded me of that first morning after the do with the ballroom-dancing farmers and the OAP jazz singer, when she told me she wanted out of London, and I staggered downstairs with a hangover and found her making lists. I recognised in her the same scared intensity.

I poured some coffee for us both, sat down and thought about whether I would miss this life or if I'd just miss it because I couldn't have it.

The thing is, whenever our world had felt threatened before, mainly when money was tight, it was the animals I panicked over. I loved them. I couldn't bear to think of losing them. But they were just part of the lifestyle. An important part, but a part just the same, while the bulk of our life was everything else. I wanted to know if I'd miss the lifestyle itself, miss living on Exmoor and being in the countryside.

Debbie balled some paper and threw it in the fire. "No!" she yelled, head back down over a clean sheet, pen scribbling.

I'd lost London, lost my job. I hadn't been happy for a while, the commute was a drag, and sometimes I'd

211

fantasise about what it would be like to live at home all the time. Even so, to get the boot, to be told I'm no longer wanted, no longer any use, "Please don't come back", hurt.

"No. Come on . . ." Debbie said, hurling another scrunched-up page into the fire. I watched her start again, scribbling, concentrating.

Yet I hadn't just lost my job. I'd lost the farm, too. We can't survive without money — nobody can. Would I miss this world we'd created? I knew I'd miss the animals, but would I miss all the bits that went with it? You know, for all the moaning, I think I would. Yes, I would, and I don't think I'm just saying that because now I can't have it. I really think I'll miss it. That's typical. That's my life in a sodding nutshell. All the while I don't want what I have, I've got it, and as soon as I do want it, it's taken away from me.

Head still down, Debbie said, "No? No. But . . . no." Balled, into the fire, restart.

We'd have to sell up and move back to London. I'd have to become a full-time vegetarian . . .

"Simon?"

I'd live on aubergines. I would be the Aubergines Man . . .

"Simon!"

But I had a Debbie. I got up and made my way over to her. She showed me the page with columns of scribbled figures. "You're right," she said. "Even with the most creative accounting possible, there's no way. The figures are too far out. The animals would starve and so would we. We will have to sell up and go back."

212

"What? I thought you'd solve it?"

"I can't magic money." Her eyes were leaking tears, but she wasn't sobbing or hysterical. She was just sad.

And so was I.

We went to bed early and comforted each other. I've never made love with both of us crying before, wiping away each other's tears and trying to smile. It's very different and very intimate.

In the morning I got up first. I had an idea. If I could get one magazine article published, then maybe I could get more. I sat down at the computer, wrote spiky article ideas to all the magazines I knew and emailed them to the editors. But I needed something more regular. Something we could budget for. So I wrote an idea for a weekly lifestyle column and emailed it to our local newspaper, the *North Devon Journal*.

Within minutes the editor responded. Okay, he said, give me an example of what you'd write.

"Oh my God." I read the email again, this time with my hands on my head in case my brain exploded. It still said the same thing. "Oh my *God!*" I ran and got Debbie.

"Will they pay you?" she said.

"Of course they will, if they like what I write."

"Well, write something good."

I wrote a short piece about the night I brought the poorly piglet up, turning our lounge into a temporary overnight cottage hospital and sitting there, trying to be quiet and not laugh so it could sleep. Then I emailed it to him.

Inbox: I new email.

From: The North Devon Journal

Message: Hi Simon, I like it — very funny. We should meet. Can you come to my office?

I scrubbed myself in the bath, shaved, drenched myself in deodorant and body spray (I had cuddled up with Kylie last night, after all), put on my best suit, considered myself in the mirror, decided it was too formal and took it off. I pulled on jeans and took them off again. Too casual. Finally I settled on smart trousers and a shirt. Yes. Then I left.

In his office, he offered me the position of weekly columnist with enough money to make me smile, but not jump up and down. I drove home like a lunatic. Debbie was back at the table, more paper, more lists, more crumpled pages in the grate.

We reworked the figures, this time together.

"So, if you can get two magazine articles a month, plus the newspaper column, and we do a farmers' market every Saturday, sell meat over the Internet and a few other bits and pieces such as eggs, we can just about break even on bills and animal feed," she surmised, pushing back her chair. "That's the good news. The bad news is there's nothing left over for us. Our disposable income to pay for all our food, clothes, toiletries, absolutely everything for you and me, is five pounds a week, if we're lucky."

"Blimey."

"Yeah, blimey is right. Mobile phones will have to go. We won't be able to afford to go to the launderette anymore either."

"How will we wash our clothes?"

She shrugged. "In the bath, I suppose. We can make bread and butter and all that. We have meat and vegetables — I guess we're part-way there already. No new books to read, of course."

"*What?* Oh no, I've got to have books," I said, feeling far worse about losing out on the books than I did the phone.

She held up her hands. A new book was a week-and-a-half's household money.

"However, the more we can save on the bills, the more we'll have for ourselves. First thing we're going to do is trash the kettle and toaster. They cost a fortune to run. If we want toast, we'll have to use a toasting fork in the fire, and we can boil a kettle on the hob."

"So we're going for it?" I asked.

"Yes — does that make you unhappy? You seem pleased with the column and the writing."

"I don't want to be a full-time farmer," I said.

"No, I know you don't, but —"

"But I don't mind being a part-time farmer and a part-time writer. Even if we are broke."

"And you won't miss London?"

It was a good question. "I hate the thought that I'm not wanted there anymore. But I guess I don't really fit in the way I used to. I don't think I'm really an estate agent anymore, you know, in the way that people are what they are: an accountant acts and looks like an accountant, and a dentist acts and looks like a dentist. Well, I don't think I look and act like an estate agent anymore. Too many things have happened. Yesterday, when I first told you I'd lost my job and you went off and started writing lists and we were both convinced we'd have to sell up, I wondered whether I'd miss the lifestyle. I knew I'd miss the animals, but I wanted to know if I'd miss the lifestyle, too. And I would. I would have gone on working in London, and I'm sure things would have been easier financially. It wouldn't have felt easy, though. Isn't it funny how when one option closes, something else opens up? Who would've thought I'd have a newspaper column?" I couldn't keep the grin off my face. "Anyway, how do *you* feel about it?"

"Scared about the money. Really scared. It's the stupid things: how am I going to buy tampons, lipstick or hairspray — how am I going to get my hair cut? What if I need tights or razors to shave my legs? I know they're all girly things, but I am a girl. I don't want to stop being feminine." I could relate to that. Not about being feminine, obviously, but about not shutting off the bits of yourself that make you you.

"Are you sure you want to do this? I mean, we could sell up and things would be a heck of a lot simpler."

"Oh, I definitely want to do it, but at the same time I'm really scared."

CHAPTER
TWENTY-NINE

London turned her back on me, so I turned my back on her. I thought that, for the first time since we moved down, I'm independent, I'm free. Okay, I was also flat broke and petrified. But at least I had a nice area to be scared in. Since I lost Bobby, I'd hardly ridden. Something about her waiting to see me before she got ready to die made me feel guilty and bad, and I couldn't get past that. But today I needed to ride. I tacked up Georgie and tied Pandy next to a hay net in her stable. Then I rode out onto the moor.

I didn't gallop or trot, I just walked. And I thought. The trouble is, there are so many things we need to have in place so that we can live without money, and they all cost. The irony is if you have money you can live without it, but if you don't have money, you need to get money before you can live without it. Catch-22. We needed a better website. We needed marketing. We needed leaflets and business cards for the market stall so people would feel confident buying our meat. Clearly, the weekly market stall was crucial. That was our cash flow to buy all the animal feed for the week. If we had a bad market, we'd have to beg, steal and borrow to get the feed another way, but which way? Where else could we turn? It was a worrying prospect.

After a while I started working Georgie, bending her, softening her and, when I felt she was ready, nudged her into a nice collected canter, all the time pushing her up into the bridle by getting her to use her bum as the engine as opposed to all the power coming from her front legs. It looks and feels beautiful when it's working well; it's hard physical work, though. After 10 minutes I was soaked in sweat — like after an hour's workout in the gym.

I rode Georgie back, the physical exertion leaving me feeling good, even if I hadn't resolved any of the issues in my head. They were a little clearer, though. Not that that made me feel any better about the situation. In fact, it made me feel worse. A problem mulled over is a problem brought into sharp focus. I prefer my problems blurred.

Debbie concentrated on the kitchen side of home: on food, drink, storing and preserving all our produce, and eking out everything; and I learned how to be practical, something that is completely alien to an estate agent. I learned how to use a sewing machine by watching videos on YouTube and asking Debbie's mum for lessons to make and mend clothes and anything fabric . . .

"How's my pretty dressmaker today?" Debbie teased. She can be really irritating at times.

I gave her my meanest boxer's dark and moody stare from my repertoire of stares. "Say that again and I'll smother you in your sleep. I'm a tailor, not a dressmaker, okay?"

"Oooh, shall we go looking at fabrics together? It'll be *such* fun!" she said, bobbing up and down with her hands clenched in front of her face, before squealing, turning and running away when I made a pretend lunge for her.

"Coward," I called.

Besides, my tailoring — t-a-i-l-o-r-i-n-g — wasn't up to much. I could do a few basics, make some clothes and things such as slippers for us both (the slippers made from an old pair of jeans looked cool), even underwear (have you any idea how difficult it is to make girls knickers? They're a nightmare: all those panels, and the elastic's either too tight and threatens to cut off circulation to Debbie's legs, or too loose and she'd spend the day preying they wouldn't flop down to her ankles). And of course patches — oh, you should see my patches! The fashion had a certain style, a certain chic, one that we wouldn't be arrested for, but I didn't live in fear of being poached by a fashion house either.

I cut all the wood for the fire myself, our only source of heating in the home, and carved things like wooden spoons and eggcups. If we needed anything, the first thing we did was try and make it.

Few things we made were catastrophic; then again, few things were brilliant. Most were just okay. Useful and usable. The biggest problem was the animal houses as there is always something in need of upgrade or repair. It was a challenge. I could only afford to buy nails and screws. Everything else I had to make or find. When the chicken-house roof collapsed, I got an old double-glazed window from a recycle centre and fitted that. It worked, a sort of coop skylight.

It would have been impossible to turn off my London eyes and no longer see everything with that desire to look nice and have attractive things around me, but I did manage to skew the vision a bit. Things became attractive in a different way. Things became beautiful because they were personal and home-made and had stories behind them. Things made me smile that would make other people turn up their noses. Mostly, I stopped comparing everything with London. Which helped. A lot.

Yet it was our secret. We never told a soul. To the outside world, everything was as it had been. All the thrift happened behind closed doors, and we went to crazy lengths to hide it because, although we understood it, we knew nobody else would. Be honest: if you went round to someone's house and every piece of clothing they had on had a patch somewhere on it (I told you I was good at patches), and all their furniture was cobbled together, would you want to associate with them? Of course you wouldn't. We want to associate with beautiful and successful people. That's human nature. So we had clothes that we kept for best, or at least we could run and change into if someone knocked at the door.

I lived in fear of someone knocking at the door.

You know the naked dream? When you dream you're in a supermarket or a shopping centre and you suddenly look down and you're naked? Well, my variant on that was to look down and I was clothed.

"Is that a knock at the door?" I whispered one night about four months after getting sacked. It was now the very depths of winter and pitch black outside most of the time. The curtains were long closed, and we were relaxing in front of the fire.

"I didn't hear anything. Wait . . ."

We heard the unmistakable sounds of the front door opening and a voice calling out hello.

"Christ!" We bumped into each other rushing to get upstairs and change when a face looked into the lounge. The face wore a smile.

"Ziggy, you prat," I said, walking back down the stairs and hugging him, while Darcy, who had been fast asleep, jumped off the sofa, bounded up to him and launched himself upright so his front paws landed on Ziggy's shoulders and he rested his chin on top of Ziggy's head, a welcome reserved for only his favourite guests. "What are you doing here?"

"What's with the harlequin costume? Have I interrupted some kinky role play?" he said, peering around the dog.

I looked down at my jeans covered in different coloured patches. "No. You know, work clothes, just not changed yet."

Debbie came down. She had changed. She gave Ziggy a kiss and started fussing over him, offering food and drink. Luckily he'd brought wine — we were still trying to perfect our home-made concoctions and wouldn't want to inflict it on anyone who valued their stomach lining, or their eyesight.

When he went up to the loo, Debbie looked at me and mouthed, "Did you know he was coming?"

I mouthed back, "No."

"What's with all the clothes in the bath?" he yelled down.

I screwed my face up. "Nothing. Just rinsing them . . . after . . . it rained earlier."

Debbie shook her head at me. I mouthed, "Well, I don't know!"

We chatted and drank his wine (after four months of nail-varnish remover, it was startlingly good), while he explained he was on the run from a recent divorcee who'd taken a shine to him, and her muscle-head jealous ex-husband. Ziggy was often cast in the role of the man who made husbands jealous and had a knack of shoring up the rocks beneath the wobbliest of marriages simply by playing the horny fool, a role for which he was naturally gifted. So good was he at repairing dodgy marriages that he was thinking of going for lottery funding.

"This one isn't my fault," he complained. "I can't help it if she's fallen in love with me, can I?" Debbie rolled her eyes. I grinned. "I need to hide. Can I crash here for a couple of nights? I tried to call, but your mobiles aren't responding."

"Oh, we lost them."

"Both of them?"

"Mm. Another drink? So tell me about her — you do know you're going to have to grow up at some point, don't you?" Debbie said, reaching for the bottle.

We turned off the TV and listened to some of Ziggy's woes. He has a lot of them. There's nothing like hearing the problems of someone who's having a really bad time to cheer you up about your own life. Sadly, he wasn't having *that* bad a time, but I still felt better when I went up to bed.

The next day I took him around the farm. We collected Dex from the barn, but left the quad bike where it was.

"Are you going to make me walk?" he moaned. I was, as the bike had no fuel in it.

"I'm sorry about Bobby," he said halfway down the hill, putting a hand on my shoulder. "She loved you to bits."

Please don't. I can't do that yet. I just can't. I took a deep breath, let it out and told him about Pandy.

"Let me guess . . . she hates you?"

"She does! She's completely different from Bobby, and that's a good thing. She hates me, but she's starting to come around. I think she'll be okay."

"So you're a proper country gent now. No more nipping off to London for work."

"No." The "no" was loaded with enough emotion to blow up a city.

"You miss it?"

I told him I did, but not often, not as much as I thought I would. But I never miss the whole package of London, just bits of it, and not always the same bits. The other day, I had this craving to walk down the high street. Nothing else, just walk down it. And I'm always feeling the urge to hold a pen.

He didn't ask how we were surviving financially. He didn't have to, it was written all over his face. I tried to write all over mine, Bugger off, it's none of your business. But I did tell him about the farmers' markets and writing a column in the local newspaper and the odd magazine article, figuring he could fill in the gaps. I guess he did because he was the one who moved the subject on.

"How're the pigs?"

"The General is such a dude. He still adores his favourite sow, really worships the mud she wallows in, but she gives him such a hard time."

"I've heard of women like that. Never met one, of course, but heard of them."

"Yeah, well, we're not all walking gigolos." A thought that reminded me of Red. "White, the cockerel, is doing okay and doing his thing, but he's a plodder compared with Red."

"Everyone's a plodder compared with Red."

"And we've got a wild boar, Geraldine. Actually, if you're here for a couple of days, you can help me move the General in with her. He'll like that, a fresh, wild, untamed woman. Makes a change from getting the cold shoulder all the time."

The next day we moved the General in, expecting foreplay between him and Geraldine to be a vicious fight before they made passionate love on a bed of their own blood, but he's so lovely: he seduced her with his porcine charm, had her eating out of his trotter and lying back, thinking of . . . England?

224

When Ziggy left, I went up into his room and found 100 pounds on the bed and a note saying it was for bed and board. What a prat. What a wonderful, wonderful prat.

I must tell you about washing clothes in the bath. One load takes a day to do, a whole day and it's hard work. It goes like this: pile the clothes into the bath and fill with warm water, swish and leave for an hour. That's the prewash. Empty and refill, this time with detergent. Then swish and agitate, poke and rub the clothes for another hour, working them all the time. I tell you, your forearms are agony. Empty the bath and squash the clothes against the sides until most of the water has run off. Then refill with clean water and swish about to rinse. Empty, refill, rinse. And again, empty, refill, rinse. Once more, this time adding conditioner. Empty and wring out the clothes. To me, washing machines are an honest-to-goodness demigod. Walking past electrical stores I want to throw myself on the floor in front of them and wail a bit. Luckily, I haven't had any near-death experiences recently, so my underwear is okay. But it's only a matter of time. For that reason I try and avoid white boxer shorts where possible.

CHAPTER
THIRTY

A week after Ziggy left, we received a phone call from someone wanting to buy meat. Internet sales had been steady, but not exciting, so a new order to go out by courier was welcome. The lady ordered and gave her name: it was Jade Goody. She had become famous in the TV show *Big Brother* and, sadly, now was famous for having been diagnosed with cancer.

She was lovely on the telephone, and she and Debbie chatted for ages. She told Debbie her oncologist at the hospital had recommended she avoid any additives in her diet. She contacted us because all our meat is additive free. She placed a big order of sausages, bacon and loads of meaty treats. She told Debbie she was going to be on the front page of the newspapers the following day. Debbie asked her how she felt about it. She said she was pleased. She said she knew she only had a short time left, and she wanted to get as much money together for her sons as she could, and that only came if she was in the headlines.

The next day we got the newspapers. Jade was right, she was all over them. She'd been having lots of chemotherapy, and the photographs splashed of her on the front pages were the first shots of her without her hair.

I didn't write about Jade in my newspaper column, but I tended to write about everything else. Every Friday morning I'd get up and write about the biggest thing that had happened with the animals that week, the funny stuff, the sad stuff, the crazy, the odd and the downright weird. At the end of each month I'd send in my invoice.

The money from the column paid for the household bills, rent, electricity, etc., while the farmers' market money paid for the animals. Anything left over was for us. Only there wasn't ever anything left over. If we needed something, we did without. If we *really* needed something, we'd beg, borrow or steal. February 11th, three days before Valentine's Day, I stole some money from our meagre kitty. I really needed something. Two somethings actually.

"Ducks!" Debbie exclaimed, peering into the box I had handed her on Valentine's Day morning. "You love me enough to buy me two baby ducks!"

That sounded odd even to me. I smiled and told her I did. The thing is you get so far down the line you think, what's two extra tiny duck mouths to feed? In the grand scheme of things it was nothing, and, besides, Debbie had been after baby ducks for ages.

As winter gradually hinted that spring might be around the corner, my brother and my mother, the very people who sacked me just six months earlier, phoned up to say they were coming down for a few days' holiday.

"I'm not sure I can do it," Debbie confessed. "I mean we've been in this house for seven years now, and your brother has never been down before. I know they're your family and everything, but the timing is really bad."

I shrugged. "I suppose I was always going up to them. They didn't need to come down and see me."

"Still, I don't think I can do it. And we certainly can't afford it. Can you imagine your brother turning up in his brand new Porsche and we can't even afford to put the kettle on to make him a coffee? I couldn't do it — I wouldn't *want* to do it. I'd say something about how they dumped you, and then it would cause problems between them and me, and probably between you and me, too. It's not a good idea. Please, can you tell them no at the moment? Maybe later, when we're on our feet a bit more, but not now."

I told them yes. I know, I know. I think I thought I could punish them if they saw how much we were struggling. Make them feel guilty for outing me. Besides, beneath the struggle I was proud of what we'd achieved and what we'd done. We had a smallholding, we had animals, we made all our own food and did everything ourselves, we laughed every day, and we were happy. I didn't even miss London. We were broke, but money's not everything. Most important, we'd found a way to survive. I am not ashamed of how Debbie and I live, and I wanted my family to be part of it. It's different when it's family. So I said yes, come down, come and spend some time in our world. They said they would and promptly booked two luxury rooms in a four-star hotel close by in Lynmouth, one for my mother and one for my brother and his family.

Debbie yelled at me, then refused to utter a word for days.

When she did start talking to me again, she said, "I am not going to be a poor relation. If they're coming, I want my hair done, I want new clothes, I want you to have new clothes, too, and I want the house to be normal. I don't want to hide our life, but I want them to see it nicely. Okay?"

I asked her where we were going to get that kind of money.

"We'll have to use the rent and electricity money."

"We can't! We'd never, ever catch back up."

"I don't care. I am not going to be a poor relation."

I pointed out, "But we are a poor relation."

She huffed and stormed off.

So that's what we did: we spent the rent and electricity money. We put lemonade, beer and bottles of wine in the fridge. We had expensive coffee brewing. Debbie had her hair done and looked lovely. We both had new clothes. We scrubbed and scrubbed and re-scrubbed the house. We washed the quilts that covered the sofas and bathed the dog. When they arrived, they came in two cars, mum in her Jaguar and brother in a shiny new 4x4 — sadly, they couldn't fit his family in the Porsche.

I'd decided long ago that I was not going to talk about the office.

"How's the office?" I said as soon as they walked through the door.

"Oh, you know . . ." my brother said.

No, I don't! I don't know because you dumped me, remember?

I smiled, nodded, offered them a drink and avoided Debbie's eyes.

I showed them around the land and introduced them to the animals, and while we were walking back through one of the fields, my little seven-year-old nephew came up and held my hand.

"Uncle Simon," he said, "It doesn't matter that it's dirty down here, does it? It doesn't matter because it's different where you live, isn't it? It's very different, so it doesn't matter . . . that it's dirty, I mean. It doesn't matter, does it?"

Oh, gee, thanks! "Um, I don't think it's that dirty, is it?"

He shook his head. "I don't think so, no."

The words had my mother all over them. I looked across at her and smiled. I was doing a lot of smiling. So was Debbie. Smile, smile, smile.

I think I wanted them to like my way of life and my animals and my home, the quad bike and Exmoor, my pigs Kylie, the General and Geraldine, the wild boar, my dog Dex, the sheep, the whole mob. I wanted so much for them to like it that, no matter what reaction they gave, I was always going to be disappointed.

I was more than disappointed: I was gutted. They didn't seem to like any of it, not even Dex and he tried the hardest, dashing about and doing everything he could think of to make them laugh. They didn't laugh.

Back at the house they didn't want beer, wine or even any of the expensive coffee. We sat in the lounge, and I lit a fire. They all perched on the edge of seats looking uncomfortable and immaculate, and even in my new clothes I felt shabby next to them. They talked about their city lives and work, staff and customers, and I thought, I miss London. I miss the office. I don't want to be a farmer. I had an urge to walk upstairs and have a bath there and then even though I knew I was clean. I wanted to put on a suit. I wanted to hold a pen. All the talk that I didn't feel as though I fitted in anymore, that I didn't feel like an estate agent, evaporated. I am an estate agent. I am every inch an estate agent.

Debbie caught my eye and frowned hard at me. I hate it when she can read my thoughts.

Part of me thought, what's wrong with me that I can't be satisfied with this wonderful, healthy, natural world that we'd created? Am I that shallow that I'd prefer to live in London the way everybody else lives? And I answered, yes, I would. But only right now, only while I had that other life staring me in the face. As soon as they'd gone, I'd be better. That's when the other part of me made a suggestion. It probably wouldn't be a good idea for me to go off and visit London for a while.

They didn't come back to the farm or the house after that, and we met them each day at their hotel. When they left, my brother gave me a hug and told me how lucky I was to live here. "You're very lucky," he said. "The kids haven't stopped talking about the animals."

He told me he'd booked to come back for New Year. I looked across at Debbie. Smile, smile, smile.

I couldn't work it out. I thought they'd hated it. Why did they want to come back for New Year? To torment me? To hurt me further? Cause me more pain and confusion? How cruel. As they drove away and we stood there waving, I handed Debbie the cheque mum had given me. I said, "Mum said she knew the effort we'd been to and that we couldn't afford it, so she gave me this." It was more than enough money to cover the rent and electricity.

CHAPTER
THIRTY-ONE

With the weather now really warming up, there was one last job to do before the summer hit, and it involved the sheep. We needed to bring them in, and as we'd been sharing fields for the sheep with Steph and they were still up at her place, Debbie and I traipsed up to help her round them all up.

The plan was that Steph's guests would create a human tunnel for the sheep to run along, with me at the end as the backstop, forcing the sheep into a stable where we could medicate them ready for the summer.

I was the only man and I was showing off — well, you would, wouldn't you? A couple of the girls chased the sheep out of the field, while I told jokes and funny stories and entertained the girlies. Then we got into position.

The sheep ran down the human tunnel towards the backstop, me.

Like a goalkeeper facing a penalty I hunkered down, arms out, bobbing left and right, ready to encourage the sheep into the stable next to me where they could be sorted.

The sheep ran towards me.

I bobbed quicker.

The sheep ran faster.

Six feet away, the lead sheep launched itself right off the ground and up into the air at me. With my arms still outstretched I didn't have time to cover my face. It took off, put its head down and smashed the top of its hard, bony skull into the soft, squashy middle of my face, hitting me with such force that I took off backward in a full Fosbury flop, landing with a solid thud on the ground. I knew my nose was broken, but even through the tears — that's what happens when you break your nose, your eyes come out in sympathy and well up — I watched the fleecy underbellies of the sheep and they all took turns running over the top of me.

When they'd all passed over, I sat up. I had dirty hoof prints up my legs and on my top and blood splattering my face. But it's okay, there were a dozen women there, they'd look after me. I was in safe female caring hands. They'd be worried I was hurt. They'd all rush over to me. Any second now. Fuss me. Mother me . . . Okay, where the hell were they?

Then the laughter hit me like a tsunami. Apparently, they couldn't make it over to me because they were too busy holding in the pee that threatened to burst if they laughed anymore. To make matters worse, I hadn't expected a near-death experience and had white underwear on. I hate it when that happens.

CHAPTER
THIRTY-TWO

"Gary Rhodes? The chef?" I said aloud.

Debbie moved the phone to the other ear and wagged her hand at me to shush. I read the scrap of paper again on which she's hastily scribbled:

Gary Rhodes wants us on his show!!!!!!!!!!

I sat on the sofa, listened to her side of the conversation and stroked my nose. This had become something of a habit since the low-flying sheep broke it. It was comforting to check it was still straight even though secretly I would have quite liked it to be more wonky. Someone with an obvious broken nose always has an air of bravery about them, and I wouldn't be above saying I sustained it in the defence of a beautiful woman, although I could only do this when Debbie wasn't around as she's not above telling people the truth, which kind of spoils the effect.

I gathered Debbie was talking to a TV researcher, and the gist of the conversation ran along the lines that Gary Rhodes, the celebrity chef, had chosen us as one of 10 finalists to represent our region of the country in his search for Britain's Local Food Hero.

I stroked my nose faster, needing more comfort.

A TV crew were on standby and would be despatched soon.

A film crew. Filming. On our land. I needed to polish the animals. I ran through the list:

The General Lee, the pig daddy

Kylie pig

Geraldine, the wild boar

Four more sows

Piglets of various ages

Georgie and Pandora, the horses

White, the cockerel, and his chicken wives

Two baby ducks

Terrorist geese

Lucky-Turkey-Leaky

Darcy, the mummy's boy Great Dane

Dex, the superstar collie dog

Flying, head-butting sheep

That's a lot of polishing.

She put down the phone. "Wow," she said.

The thing is, people watching TV expect animals to be beautifully pristine, when the reality is all my pigs want to spend their days lazing about and snoozing in muddy puddles.

"I need to polish my pig," I said out loud.

Debbie started smiling. "You boys . . . Is it the way I was standing?"

"No . . . No! I need to polish the pigs if a film crew are coming here to film us. Nobody's going to want to see mucky pigs. When are they coming?"

"Next Wednesday." She explained that someone had recommended us to the programme and they'd put up our details on their website where people could vote for who they wanted to see on the show based on ethics and resulting produce. We, apparently, were really popular.

"So we're going to be on TV?" I said, hating the fact that whenever I get stressed I start spouting the obvious. TV. We were going to be famous. The whole country was going to see our farm and our pigs and our way of life — thank goodness we'd bought some new clothes.

Debbie said, "They want to film down on the land and then film me cooking some of our pork for Michael Caines."

"My name is —"

She cut me off. "He's a chef. Two Michelin stars. I'm going to be cooking for a two-star Michelin chef. *Aaaahhhhhhh!*" She rolled back on the sofa and waved her feet in the air she was so excited.

"I thought it was Gary Rhodes?"

She stopped waving her feet. "He's back at the studio and sends out top chefs as his eyes and ears, and they report back to him."

I thought of all the polishing I'd have to do, not just the animals but the land, too. Spring is a scruffy time of year when stinging nettles and thorns grow and threaten to take over the place, and there's mud and rain, and it all just makes you daydream of concrete (if I ever win the lottery, not that I do it, I'm going to install a giant movable canopy over the entire land that opens when it's sunny and closes when it rains. Oh yes, I've got big plans). I wish I still had Bobby, she was *so* photogenic. And Red . . . on second thoughts maybe not Red — he's not exactly family viewing.

For the next five days I cleaned the land, fixed anything that needed fixing, tidied up, strimmed everything into neatness, refreshed bedding, cleaned water buckets and feed troughs. At home, we scrubbed the kitchen and disassembled all the self-sufficiency bits of our life that weren't fun and quirky but rather mundane and a tiny bit sad, such as the bucket of mushrooms and nettles steeped in water under the kitchen table (I was using it to dye one of Debbie's old blouses yellow) or the toasting fork in front of the fire with which we made toast. I replaced them with a cheese press and butter paddles and tidily lined up pots of homemade jams, chutneys and infused oils on the shelves.

The film crew arrived, and I felt good. The effort I'd put into the animals and the land showed, and it all gleamed — you could almost see your own reflection in the pigs. The director and the cameraman arrived in the same car. I went out, shook their hands and cracked a joke, which for once didn't fall flat, and tried my best to be jovial. Then the cameraman uncovered the camera. It was one of those huge TV cameras that they carry on their shoulders. I looked at it and literally wobbled.

"Are you okay?" one of them asked. "For a second there I thought you were going to fall over."

So did I. I'd like to have told them that, but my tongue had come out in sympathy and lolled uselessly against my teeth. The sight of the camera had sent terrified, unsettling Shockwaves through my mouth and body. I tried to tell myself that the camera wasn't even on, let alone on his shoulder. It was on the back seat of the car switched off. But none of the bits inside me that controlled logic were listening. In all the time that I had been preparing for this, I hadn't once considered what it would be like to stand with a camera pointing at me. I did it now, and I didn't like how it felt — it felt . . . wobbly.

I tried to picture my face, the one I looked at when I shaved each morning in order to superimpose it onto a television screen, but I couldn't for the life of me remember what I looked like, and I wasn't at all sure I wanted to. From the little I could remember I thought my face was okay, as faces go, but there was just a lot of it because of my receding hairline, and everyone knows lots of face is unattractive, unless you're Sean Connery.

But I could have put up with that. What worried me more was what came out of my face — in other words, my voice. I was going to have to speak and say things that would be recorded and played back on television for millions of people to listen to. It was a horrible thought. I knew that some of the time I said things that were interesting. I also knew that some of the time I said things that were boring. The problem was most of the time I talked drivel. I wanted to avoid the drivel, and if at all possible, I wanted to avoid the boring things, too. It was a tall order.

"Hoffee hor hea?" I said, my tongue still not working, so I backed it up with the universal mime for drinking.

The cameraman laughed. Maybe it wasn't the first time he'd seen this reaction to his camera. We went into the kitchen, and I put the kettle on and made drinks, while Debbie chatted through the shots they wanted to capture. It was a while before Michael Caines arrived to the throaty rumble of a Porsche engine that swept into the farmyard, and came in shaking hands and kissing Debbie on the cheek. You never know with chefs how they're going to be, but he's a really nice, down-to-earth guy.

Having established they wanted piggy shots, I said, "I'm really looking forward to you meeting my pigs."

The silence wasn't long, but it was very wide. "Are you?"

I should have known to bail out then, but I didn't. "Oh yeah," I enthused. "There's the General, he's a great lad, very handsome. And Kylie, she's such a pretty girl. Then there's the hooligans, they're the piglets. And adolescents, they're hooligans, too, only a bit older, and some other sows, and, and . . ." I'd lost their interest. They were all leaning over a clipboard mumbling, and I felt silly the way you do when your audience collectively finds something more interesting to do than listen to you, and I wasn't even talking drivel.

It was clear from the outset they were favouring Debbie and wiping me out of all the shots. I felt both relieved and annoyed. I didn't want to be in it, but I quite liked the idea of them kneeling in front of me pleading and begging just to show a little of me — pretty, pretty please? They didn't. All the talk was,

"Debbie, while we film, could you do . . ." or "Debbie, would you be able to . . ." I carried on making the drinks, trying to remember who had milk and sugar.

At one point Debbie took me into a quiet corner and asked if I was okay with her doing the work, and I thought of how I wobbled looking at the camera. I assured her I was more than fine with it.

When they pronounced they were happy with the plan of action and started gathering their bits and pieces together, I took hold of Debbie's arm and pulled her close to my side. "So," I said, beaming, "Do we look okay?"

They looked at each other without moving their heads, a trick that takes practised pairs of eyes. "Urn, yes . . . ?"

I meant it to show that we were together, that we came as a pair. Debbie pulled away, giving me a look that said, why the hell are you acting like such a prat?

I leant against the nearest wall, smiled and tried to look relaxed while mentally duffing myself up.

CHAPTER
THIRTY-THREE

Cameraman, director, two-Michelin-star chef Michael Caines and tons of kit all bundled into our vehicle, and Debbie drove them down, while I clambered on the quad bike. By the time I got down to the chicken field, they were already attaching hidden microphones to Debbie's clothes. "Sorry we can't mike you up, too, Simon, it's just that we only have one microphone pack with us." I looked at their bags. Families with small children go on a fortnight's holiday with less kit than they had.

Debbie took Michael Caines over to the pigs and introduced them one by one. She was so natural and relaxed you'd never have known there was a camera a hand's width away from her face. They chatted, and he asked questions and she answered with enthusiastic funny stories. I was so proud of her.

As the conversation continued, the cameraman decided to do a long sweeping shot all the way around us to establish where we were in the woods. Just as he began to pan away, the General considered it was all getting rather boring and he might as well have sex. He nudged Kylie in a friendly, "fancy a bit?" manner and reared up behind her.

242

Everyone knew what was going on except the cameraman.

Debbie and Michael stared in horror, but kept talking. The producer started silently laughing, shaking his head and indicating to me if I could do something about it.

Unable to shout out that he was a dirty bugger and to get off her, I looked around for something to hit him with, grabbed a bucket and began whacking him on the back with it, but rather than find this annoying and stop, he set his rhythm by it.

I'm whack, whack, whacking him, and he's thrust, thrust, thrusting, the producer's biting his own knuckle to keep the laugh from bursting out, Debbie and Michael are still talking . . .

". . . all the feed is locally milled and is very low in . . ."

. . . I'm still whacking, the General's still thrusting, Kylie's loving every second of all the attention, and the cameraman, still oblivious, is now halfway round his slow arc.

I had to do something. I put down the bucket and moved behind the General, figuring I'd physically drag him off her. I put my arms around his neck and lowered myself onto his back.

It was humiliating. As he bucked back and forth, so did I. I was gripping either side of the General's head, my arms at full stretch leaning back and my face turning red with the excursion of trying to pull him away, while my hips humped back and forth in time with his. I was humping and groaning with the effort,

243

he was humping and whimpering, with Kylie under us, moaning, and all the while I could see the camera moving around towards us.

Ménage à trois is one thing, but we were nowhere near a bed and we weren't even the same species. If I was caught on film looking like I'm . . . That's when a shot of superhuman strength burst through me. You've heard of parents ripping the car door from a burning vehicle to save their child — well, this was something like that. With a hit of intense energy surging through my muscles I managed to pull, twist and unbalance the General enough to tip him off Kylie and scamper out of the way just as the camera settled back on the pigs.

". . . so all in all they're very healthy, happy and natural pigs," Debbie concluded.

"Cut!"

I slumped down on the ground, all the strength evaporating from my legs.

"That was the funniest thing I have ever seen in my life," the producer said.

"It was. Hilarious!" Michael added.

"Oh, sweetheart," Debbie said.

"What?" said the cameraman.

I carried on slumping and said nothing. After a while, when they had all the outdoor shots they needed, we began getting ready to go back up to the house. Bags of kit were loaded back in our vehicle when the cameraman said, "Can I come up on the quad bike with you?"

"Sure." Obviously, I expected him to put the camera in the vehicle with the rest of the kit where it would be safe. Obviously. "You're bringing that on the bike?" I said, stunned when it was clear he wouldn't be parted from it, not even if he was going off-roading on a quad bike.

"I don't ever let anyone else take responsibility for it," he said.

"Okay." I got on. So did he. I was in front, he was behind, the camera wedged between us. I started the engine. "I'll drive carefully," I promised. "Incidentally, how much would it cost to replace if anything happened to the camera? Not that anything *is* going to happen."

"About £45,000."

I elected not to tell him about my safety record, the near-death experiences or the fact that I no longer wore white underwear as life around here had a tendency to become a bit nervy, and drove towards home, very slowly.

Back at the house they were deciding that Debbie should cook sausages made with our own pork, which was handy as that's what we'd prepared. Big TV lights were installed in the kitchen, and the floor was a tangle of leads. Everything was ready. Debbie had a frying pan in her hand, hovering over the hob, with sausages on a plate to one side waiting to be cooked. Beside her, Michael Caines stood ready to launch into his chat. The cameraman, tight for space, had jumped up onto the work surface and hunkered into a corner, the camera on his shoulder, lens pointed down. The producer sat at the table. He said, "Everybody ready? Okay. And . . . action —"

"Wait!" The cameraman shouted. "Simon, I can see you peeking around the door!"

I ducked back in the lounge. "Um, sorry."

"Okay. And . . . action!"

I sat on the sofa listening to Debbie talk about cooking the sausages. She was really good, but as good as she was, and as proud of her as I felt, I couldn't help wishing it was me out there with her. I felt a bit lonely, a bit Billy-no-mates-ish sitting in here on my own.

It took an hour and a half, but finally it finished. That's a wrap! It's in the can! Done and dusted! TV people do like their clichés. While the camera and equipment were packed away, Michael raved about the sausages, said how much he loved our smallholding and our animals, kissed Debbie, shook my hand and reversed his Porsche out the yard, with the producer and cameraman following soon after.

"I am exhausted," Debbie said, flopping down.

"So am I." I plonked down next to her. I wasn't exhausted. I just felt if I couldn't share the filming with her, at least I could share the aftermath. Just before she fell asleep, I whispered, "You did really well today, and I'm so proud of you."

"Mmm, you did well, too," she said as she nodded off.

CHAPTER
THIRTY-FOUR

There must be some sort of internal list TV companies use because soon afterwards we got a phone call from BBC1's *Countryfile*. The chairman of the NFU (National Farmers' Union) had come out against what he called hobby farmers, branding them a liability. *Countryfile* wanted the other side of the story. Would we be interested?

For 40 years of my life, nobody had wanted me for television, and now in quick succession two film crews were despatched and trundled into our yard. Only for the second lot, I was prepared.

I spent ages down on the farm practising. The thing is, they don't let you look into the camera unless you're the presenter because it makes the interviewee look shifty. Not looking at something is much harder than it sounds, so whenever I was out working on the farm, I'd pretend there was a camera pointing towards me and I'd talk out loud as though I were being filmed. At the start, it was really difficult. Aside from feeling stupid, self-conscious and sounding like a pompous arse, I had trouble not looking at something when I told myself I couldn't.

I'd imagine a tree was a camera and I'm not allowed to look at it. I'd stroll along with the chickens, chatting to the imaginary camera (tree) I'm not looking at, "Yes, of course, these are chickens. They lay eggs. Some of the chickens are, um, brown, as you can see. And, er, some are white and black. Christ, why do I sound so boring — I might just as well be singing a lullaby, *and now I'm staring at the damn tree!*"

It's something to do with being aware of an object in your peripheral vision, but not being able to look at it. It's like having an itch you can't scratch. It's maddening. But little by little it got easier until I was ignoring trees like a master. It became a source of pride that I could not look at anything I chose. That hedge over there, I'm not going to look at it, and I wouldn't! The fence, ha, what fence? I was like a gunslinger, walking and picking a target and rather than shoot it, I'd not look at it. Damn, I was good.

Being *Countryfile*, they arrived, as you would expect, with a big film crew and a huge black 4x4. I shook hands as we all introduced ourselves. "I'm Adam," said Adam Henson, the presenter. It must be difficult when you're famous to know how to treat a situation like that. Everyone knows Adam. He could quite legitimately grip my hand and say nothing, or say, you know who I am, but he didn't. He smiled and said, "I'm Adam."

I do get starstruck. Living on Exmoor, I only ever see my animals, my wife and the farmers' market on a Saturday. Meeting someone I recognised from the telly was amazing. I told myself not to grin, but did anyway. However, at least I didn't say anything stupid. Well,

248

actually . . . "It's going to be nice weather today," I blurted out, thinking, *no! Don't talk about the weather, you fool!* They all looked up. The sky was black.

"So, Simon," the producer said, leaning over a cup of coffee and blowing on the top of it after we'd all decamped to the kitchen, "What have you got for me?"

"I'm really looking forward to you meeting my pigs," I said.

The silence wasn't long, but it was very wide. "Are you?"

Déjà vu.

I should've known to bail out then, but I didn't. "Oh yeah," I enthused. "There's the General, he's a great lad, very handsome. And Kylie, she's such a pretty girl. Then there's the hooligans, they're the piglets. And adolescents, they're hooligans, too, only a bit bigger, and some other sows, and, and . . ."

He leant forward. "Go on."

Oh, you beauty. I took a deep breath of crisp clean air and felt any stress that I would be sidelined again drop away.

". . . and some really pretty sheep and lambs. Chickens, I can't stand the chickens, but we've got chickens —"

"You do like the chickens, you're such a liar," Debbie laughed.

"Terrorist geese, ducks . . ." I gave him the run-down of all the animals.

When I'd finished, he said great, and went on to explain that they wanted some establishing shots of us on the land with the animals, and then they wanted to talk to me about the comments made by the chairman of the NFU. Was I happy with that?

They wanted to talk to me. Not Debbie. Me. Look, if I'm going to be the star of the show, I think I deserve a Winnebago with a gold sticker on the door, a makeup girl, someone to do my hair — don't choke — wardrobe, champagne, roses that have been dipped in the life-preserving waters of a secret pool the whereabouts of which are known only to a single monk who is forbidden to pass the details on to anyone except his successor, and only then when it's been verified by three independent doctors that he has no more than an hour to live. Get your people to talk to my people . . .

"That's perfect," I said.

They went down in the 4x4 and I drove on the quad. While I gripped the handlebars and thumbed the accelerator, I thought, so what is my response to the NFU statement that hobby farmers were a liability? Well, I disagree. There, that was easy.

They filmed geese chasing chickens, and geese chasing ducks, and geese chasing Lucky-Turkey-Leaky, and geese chasing Dex, poor thing, and geese hurling abuse at me as I refused to be chased on TV. Then we made our way down to the pigs.

Conscious of what had gone before, I'd moved the General in with some boys, but it was Geraldine, the wild boar, they were most taken with. She'd given birth to four little ones who were ginger with four black stripes running along their backs tip to tail. They looked so cute.

Adam Henson was brilliant. He's a genuine, down-to-earth guy and so, so easy to get on with. No wonder he's popular. It's only when you watch someone like that work that you get to appreciate how clever and good at what they do presenters really are. For my part, I didn't wobble when I saw the camera, and I was as good at ignoring it as Adam; in fact, not wanting to split hairs, I think I might even have been a little bit better — having worked solidly on my ignoring technique, I felt I'd cracked it.

"Okay, so how about we walk through the woods with the pigs around us — will they follow us?" Adam asked.

"Oh yes," I said.

"Right. So we'll walk through the woods with the pigs, I'll ask you about the NFU comments, and you tell me what you think, okay?"

Walk and talk, that sounds dangerously close to multitasking, do I look like a girl? "Fine," I said.

"We're ready here. Everyone else?" the producer called. The soundman and the cameraman held thumbs-up signs aloft.

"Okay, here we go . . ." Adam said, pausing, looking down, then looking up at me. This was the first time he'd done a piece on camera, and in a voice I'd not heard him use before — an enthusiastic, interested, keen voice — said, "So, Simon, the chairman of the National Farmers' Union this week . . ." Apparently, the chairman of the NFU had said something along the lines that he believed hobby farmers were causing problems because they don't know what they are doing, and labelled them a liability. The cheek! ". . . what do you say to that?"

Am I supposed to speak in the same enthusiastic voice? Is that how it's done on TV? Without thinking, without meaning to, I copied him.

"Well, Adam," I said, heaping so much enthusiasm into the words that I sounded speeded up and, worst of all, looked as though I was parodying him. But I couldn't stop. Once you start enthusiastic, it's impossible to tone it down mid-sentence without coming across as though you have a fast-acting bipolar disorder that sends your moods up and down at the click of a finger. So I carried on. I could feel myself blushing. *"Well, Adam*, I don't *think* the *chairman* of the *NFU* is *correct! For instance*, when *we* took over *this land*, before *we* got any *animals*, we *went* on a *pig-keeping course!"*

"Cut! Can we try that bit again?"

Adam grinned and went to say something, but I cut him off. "Yes, I know, sorry," I said.

"And . . . action!"

He asked the question again. I thought, just imagine they're all trees and ignore them. I'm good at ignoring trees. An expert; I would say professional, but it's tough to earn a living ignoring trees these days — I blame the government, lack of apprenticeships and all that.

". . . what do you say to that?" Adam said.

"I don't agree." I breathed a sigh of relief at sounding almost human. "Smallholders and small-scale farmers — it's a bit patronising to call us hobby farmers — do it because we love our animals, and as such . . ."

I nailed it. I sounded confident, I sounded good, and I made a solid case on behalf of smallholders. I laid it on thick — how dare they call us a liability! As I did, I thought, a little while ago I was in a similar situation with television cameras around, only then I was dry-humping the General. But I didn't mention that. Neither did I mention electrocuting my testicles. Rolling the quad bike. Drowning on a gate. Breaking my nose on a sheep. Flicking horse poo onto my head. Getting a head butt in the goolies by a lamb — that's enough, I don't want to belabour the point. But to call me a liability! So I put the record straight, once and for all. Your Honour, I plead not guilty to the charge and rest the case for the defence. I am not a liability, I'm just a bit unlucky — your witness!

Food Heroes aired in the September, and *Countryfile* the following February. For a few months, we owned TV.

CHAPTER
THIRTY-FIVE

The night *Food Heroes* went out, Debbie and I cuddled together on the edge of the sofa, forcing down a few glasses of vicious-tasting dandelion Dutch Courage. Then *Gary Rhodes' Local Food Heroes* started. We were first on the show, and all of a sudden there was Debbie looking wonderful and relaxed, chatting with Michael Caines in our woods with the pigs and cooking sausages in our kitchen. Then it switched back to the studio, and Gary Rhodes cooked some of the pork we'd sent to the studio for him.

"I'm really excited about Debbie Dawson and her Hidden Valley Pigs smallholding on Exmoor," Gary Rhodes said, looking out of the television at us. "And this pork looks stunning." The episode incorporated his top six food producers for the entire south-west of England, that's six counties. The winner would go into the grand final. We didn't win, but we did come second.

I wasn't in it, only Debbie, but five months later, it was my turn.

On the morning *Countryfile* went out, I got up early and did the animals, walked the legs off Darcy, made up the fire and settled down to phone everyone I knew. I phoned Ziggy first and left a message on his voicemail. It was a Sunday morning, just a few hours after a Saturday night, which meant he would still be in bed and was unlikely to be alone. Next, I phoned my mum and my brother and Debbie's mum and Debbie's brother, all of whom promised to watch it, and then left the phone to one side while I started rummaging in the kitchen drawer.

"What are you looking for?" Debbie asked.

I told her I was looking for the Christmas card list so I could start working my way through it.

"You want to phone everyone we know?"

I stopped and looked up, my face arranging itself in a display of shock that she would even consider not doing the rounds. "Of course I want to phone everyone we know, it's not everyday you get to appear on the telly, you know."

She talked me out of it. It took a while and a lot of convincing, but eventually I gave up on the idea. With nothing to do, I paced back and forth across the lounge. I should've felt pleased that my body functioned on a level that didn't involve any conscious effort from me, because my brain had turned into a kaleidoscope of random thoughts zipping all over the place, first lighting up and demanding to be noticed before dimming off to one side only to spark up again later. Anxiety would have shut my body into a coma had Mother Nature not had the smarts to install an autopilot to cover such cases of pre-televisual stress attacks.

What if I looked like an idiot? What if they used the first overenthusiastic version? I'd be a laughing stock then. I should never have called my mum or anyone else. Thank God Debbie stopped me working my way through our friends.

I needed to calm down and quieten the noise inside my head, so I went out to the log shed and chopped some of the wood stacked up for the fire. I swung the axe, first high up over my shoulder, then down as hard as I could onto the log in front of me splitting it in two. High up, fast down, split. High up, fast down, split. It's therapeutic, calming and peaceful concentrating on the logs. High up, fast down, split. I cut enough for the week and felt nearly normal as I made my way back into the house.

"Ziggy called back. He said he's going to tape it," Debbie said, adding, "He sounded . . . distracted. I wonder who he's with?"

I shrugged. It was nearly time. I imagined friends and family would be sitting down right about now and flicking to the correct channel. I felt sick. I made up the fire again, even though it didn't need it.

Then, there I was on the television screen in our woods surrounded by our pigs, Adam Henson next to me asking his NFU question. I held my breath as I watched myself answer, then I let it out. They used the second version — I'd been consumed with worry that they'd use the first over-egged version, but they didn't, it was okay. Ha, it was okay!

"That was good," Debbie said. "You came across really well."

I felt relieved and did a little dance in the middle of the floor, Darcy jumping off the sofa and joining in. It's hard to dance with a Great Dane in a small lounge, so we stuck to a waltz. "I wasn't as good as you, but I wasn't an idiot," I said to Debbie, counting one, two, three . . . one, two, three . . . and trying not to step on Darcy's toes.

My stepmum called to congratulate us and said she was sending us a present. I asked what it was, but she wouldn't tell me, only saying I had to be in on this certain day.

"Do you know what it is?" I said to Debbie after I'd put down the phone.

"I think I might have an idea. I was talking to her, and something might have slipped out."

I closed my eyes. "What?"

"Just . . . It's okay. You'll be pleased. Wait and see — I might have it wrong, after all."

Despite threatening to give her a Chinese burn, she still wouldn't tell me, so I had no choice but to wait and see. On the day, a lorry shuddered to a halt in the lane outside and two burley guys struggled to unload an enormous box. I looked at the writing on the side. It was a washing machine. *It was a washing machine!*

CHAPTER
THIRTY-SIX

If you spend your life dicing with Death, at some point you know He's going to throw a six and you're going to throw a one. I threw a one, but it wasn't my fault. I was just unlucky. Yes, I know, unlucky again.

Barnstaple Hospital, Accident and Emergency. Bright lights, sticky atmosphere, odd smell and the worst kind of pain, which is pain that's happening to me.

"Does it hurt a lot?" Debbie said next to me, looking down at my tattered hand.

"I'm trying not to think about it," I said bravely, shifting in the cold, hard plastic chair of the waiting area and wondering how many people leave casualty with haemorrhoids.

"You shouldn't have tried to pick him up," she said, not unkindly.

"I know."

"If you did, you should've worn gloves."

"Yes, I know."

"He really savaged you — careful, you're dripping blood."

I rewrapped the makeshift bandage. Well, who do you think did it? Which little git turned into a monster and savaged me? The General, 50 stone of male pig bulging with testosterone? No, course not. A goose then? Nope. Sheep — no. Horses — no. Chickens — no. You'll never guess . . .

"Are you going to tell the doctor what happened?" Debbie asked, rubbing my arm and looking concerned.

"S'ppose."

"It's important. You will tell the truth, won't you?"

"I'm not a child."

"It's quite funny really. All the things you've done, all the scraps you've been in and you end up in hospital because of a kitten."

"*It was not a kitten!* It was a wild cat!"

"Yeah, a wild kitten called Morris."

"It doesn't make him any nicer just because he's got a name, you know."

We had decided it would be a kind thing to give a home to a couple of feral cats and contacted the Cats Protection League. Cute fluffy kittens are rehomed in a whisker, even older moggies find a loving home, but feral cats, cats that are wild, have little chance. An excited lady came out, assessed us and brought two cats with her, Morris and Nikodemus.

Next to nothing is known about either Morris or Niko except they were found in really bad condition, seem never to have had human contact and become petrified anywhere near people. They were moved about from centre to centre up and down the country for two years while staff tried to build enough trust to allow them to be picked up and fussed. But nothing they did worked. They were too far gone, too wild. You wonder what type of life they had before that made them so nervous.

Anyway, six months after they arrived with us, Morris was knocked over. I'm not sure what he was doing up on the lane in the first place (after all he's got 20 acres of woods and land, barns and sheds to muck about in), but he was running across the lane when a car hit him. Because he's feral, the only way we could catch him to gauge the extent of his injuries was to set a trap, and that's what we did. It took two weeks, but we caught him. It was clear his tail had been run over. I picked him up gently and carefully, and he just flipped and tore into my hand with teeth and claws, ripping out huge chunks of flesh so that they hung loose from my bones with paws that only hours earlier had probably been disembowelling a bird with some flu-like death virus, a bird about the size of an ostrich I should think. When he was content my hand was ripped open to its fullest extent and thoroughly contaminated, he emptied his bladder and weed all over it. It was a miracle I'd made it all the way into hospital before infection had wormed its way up my arm, into my brain and killed me stone dead.

"You can't die that quick from an infection," Debbie said. "And besides, you promised me you were going to tell the truth."

"Sorry, I didn't realise I was talking out loud — and it is the truth!"

"An ostrich?"

"Well, you don't know."

"Yes, I think I'd notice if there were ostriches living on Exmoor."

We went quiet and watched a man about my age, in suit and tie, hop to a seat several rows in front of us. I longed to wear a suit and tie and felt all the envy inside me bubble to the surface. I didn't care what job he did, I didn't care how bad his foot was; it might even need to be amputated for all I knew, but in that second I would have done anything to swap places with him. And then I thought, that's a hell of a thing to think just because he's wearing a suit! I looked down at my jeans, my rotten old work jeans covered in patches where the material beneath was ripped or frayed, and the fresh stains of blood from my hand, and closed my eyes.

Sure, we had some fun times, and I loved the animals, but those old London thoughts were beginning to nag away inside me again. I love London, what can I say? To help me focus, I did a new tally:

Niko and Morris, the kittens
Dex
The General
Kylie pig
Geraldine
Four more sows
Piglets of various ages
White, the cockerel
The girls (hens)
Two ducks
Terrorist geese
Lucky-Turkey-Leaky
Georgie and Pandora, the horses

Darcy, the mummy's boy Great Dane

Sheep and lambs

We had dropped off Morris at the vet's before coming here. It looks like he's going to have to have his tail amputated, poor thing. Can cats still jump about without a tail? Don't they use them for balance? We'll have to see how he gets on when he comes home — come to think of it, that really is the definition of bad luck, living for two years in a series of rescue centres, and as soon as you get lucky and find somewhere nice to live, you get run over. What a bitch — at least my luck's not that bad.

There are lots of reasons why I'm thinking about London. Money's a big part of it. Living on nothing is draining, and I'm worried about Debbie. As much as this life is her absolute dream, it is tough watching her build herself up to phoning the electric company and begging for more time to pay because we've just received a letter to say they're going to cut us off. I know she's thinking, I used to be one of the most successful property lawyers in South London, and now look at me.

The truth is, money affords you your own sense of worth and pride. Money doesn't *buy* you pride: it gives it away for free as a side order. But you have to have it first. Without money, you feel like dirt when the person on the other end of the phone line is saying, "Just pay 20 pounds. You must be able to pay 20 pounds," and you have to admit to yourself that they might as well be asking for 20,000. You know you cannot pay, but you try anyway and search in the back of drawers, old purses and handbags; you look around for anything you can sell, knowing that everything of any worth has already long gone; and for one short moment you even wonder if you can cut down the animals' feed a bit each day so you can save up the 20 pounds, before feeling sick that you've even considered breaking the one golden rule that must be upheld above all others: the animals never suffer and never go without.

I'm worried Debbie might be slipping into some form of deep sadness.

To top it all, following our appearance on *Food Heroes* and *Countryfile* a couple of months ago, most of our old London friends saw for the first time what our life is like, and have had a difficult time accepting it. At least half no longer stay in touch the way they had, and the other half are shaky. Ziggy's great and Paula's wonderful, but other than those two, all the old developers, solicitors and the London crowd we'd gathered around us have stopped returning our calls. It's sad, but I guess (God, I hate myself for admitting this) we now lead an 'alternative lifestyle', and many of the people we used to associate with would walk across broken glass to avoid that.

I feel the need to shave my head. Some people self-harm, but that must really hurt. Shaving my head probably has a similar motivation behind it: the desire to control something when everything else feels as though it's spinning out of control. I also need to get out of these blood-splattered jeans. I want to be in London. I want to have money and not be scared to answer the phone or open the post because people are going to scream at me for money. I want to wear a suit. I want to hold a pen. I want to talk on the phone about a house . . .

"There are three bedrooms, two double and one single, but it's the kitchen that you're going to love. Imagine the newest sleek white units with chrome handles, chrome taps, even chrome plug sockets. There's plenty of work space . . ."

But, and this is annoying, just as much as I want to be in London and be financially comfortable, I also want to spend time with Kylie. I want to talk to the General. I want to ride on the quad bike with Dex. I want to hop on Georgie and for us to disappear over the moor together, and cut wood, close the curtains, light the fire and crouch in front of it with the palms of my hands thrust as close to the flames as I can get. I even want to collect eggs. I want everything; I want it all, London *and* Devon, and I don't feel guilty for wanting everything, just frustrated.

Debbie and I need to talk about what we're going to do. We need to sit down and go through it. Should we keep the farm or sell up and move back?

"I'm not selling up and moving back!"

"Christ, was I talking out loud again?" I said. I've really got to watch that.

"You like the animals, you like the farmers' markets, you like the writing. Would you give up the magazine work and your newspaper column, because you'd have to if we moved back to London? We simply need to find a way of earning some more money. And I'm not deeply sad, I'm just tired."

"Simon Dawson!" a nurse called.

I got up. "I need to . . ." I waved my bad hand at Debbie and sent a sprinkling of tiny spots of blood onto her trousers. "Oops."

"Go! And tell the truth — you promised."

"We'll talk about it later, yes?"

"Just go and be careful," she said, searching her bag for a tissue.

I went. They were very nice and cleaned me up, injected me, bandaged my hand and wrote out a prescription for some strong antibiotics. Then I collected Debbie and we went home.

CHAPTER
THIRTY-SEVEN

Actually, we didn't go straight home from the hospital. I had my wellies in the truck and drove straight down onto the land. It's funny how you need certain interaction at certain times. There was a point in the hospital when one of the nurses reached out and touched my hand. I didn't know that's what I needed until I felt her do it (though she obviously saw something in me), but wow, it picked me up like I'd been injected with a drug.

The thing is, I do know how important physical contact is. I touch every one of my pigs every day. Just a pat or a stroke. For ages, I believed it was good for the pigs to know that they were loved and cared for, but I hadn't realised how important it had become for me.

Having spent the morning in a clinical, scrupulously clean hospital environment, what I really needed was to go down and spend some time touching and being with the pigs.

I grabbed a bucket of feed and walked into the first pen.

It was muddy and gooey and the pigs scampered over, bustling around me. I chucked some feed on a big dry patch of ground and laughed when a youngster lost his spot when one of the others squirmed underneath him and lifted him in a piggyback clean away from his food and started eating it from underneath him.

I knelt down right in the middle of the pigs. They smelt musty and earthy. Pigs can pretty much absorb any mood you're in. They're good like that. Sometimes I want to hug them, sometimes I just want to pet them. But from time to time I just need some male banter.

I touched the pigs, and I swore and I laughed and I called them dumb names. I was sarcastic and cutting, and bit by bit all the anxiety and fear that had built up in me over Morris and the hospital trip, all the worry over money and Debbie seeped away . . . well, not away exactly, but into the background. I think I just needed to let off steam. It's my equivalent of going into a working men's pub where everybody knows my name, and in just the same way the pigs gave me back as good as they took, if not more.

After 10 minutes I said I was going and made my way over to Debbie, who'd been standing off to one side. She hugged me. "You show all the signs of a normal person, but you do it in the most un-normal way. You don't do that to them every night, do you?"

I shook my head. "We're never normally boisterous with each other, but I just needed —"

"It's okay," she cut in, "I know what you needed, you needed to be a boy. It's just amazing that they knew what you needed, too."

I laughed, feeling suddenly proud of my relationship with the pigs. I thought, am I happy enough with this life to stick it out and work a way around the lack of money? I looked at the General and I looked at Kylie, and all the others, all my friends.

The drive to the hospital had used every penny we had in fuel. Everything. I could not now rub two pound coins together if my life depended on it, and the only way I was going to get more money was to do the farmers' market on Saturday. But to do the farmers' market, I had to get there. Which took fuel.

I was used to turning up at the market with empty pockets and having to earn enough money not only to pay for the stall, but also to buy enough fuel to get home, and that's without even thinking about getting animal feed for that night! Let me tell you that's the kind of pressure that makes you a good salesman. There was not a person who walked by my stall who didn't get a beaming smile and nod down to the neat rows of gorgeous homemade sausages, chops and joints in front of me.

Most of the time it would work, but sometimes, when I was tired and the pressure and the worry of it all would get to me, someone would only have to say something and I'd lose it. This one time, a lady pointed at the black pudding and asked me how much? I told her 50 pence a slice. "Fifty pence!" she said, "That's a rip-off!"

I lost it. I walked around to her side of my stall. "It's a rip-off? Have you any idea how I make it? Well, let me tell you. First off, I help deliver the pig, act as midwife, you know? Then I feed, water and tuck it in every night for eight or nine months, worrying about it, stressing over it, making sure it's happy. Then early one

268

morning, I load it into a trailer and I drive it to the abattoir. I watch it being killed, I watch the slaughter man stun it, winch it up into the air and dig a knife into its neck, nicking the Carotid artery, and while it's going through its death throws, I hold onto its ear and point the stream of blood that's shooting out of it into a bucket. Then I take the blood home, process it, cook it, slice it and bring it here. Now please tell me, is 50 pence a slice really a rip-off?"

She went so pale I thought she was going to pass out.

I think back to the start when we left London and moved down, although it felt complicated at the time, the decision to stay or move back to London would have been a lot easier to make than it is now. Now I wonder if I'll ever make a decision, and sometimes I wonder if there's even a decision to be made. I think about the General and I think about Kylie. I look at the rest of the animals, and I think, they're all my best friends; could I really turn my back on them? But I turned my back on my London friends and moved away from those. So what's the difference? Actually, we'll treat that as a rhetorical question because I really can't start looking into who I'm closer to, the animals or my old friends, because I'm scared it would come out as the animals. That would make me weird, and I don't want to be weird, I want to be normal. *Tum, de tum, de tum, de tum.* "Talk to me," I said, turning away from the pigs finishing the snack I'd put in for them to look at Debbie.

"Let's go back up to the house," she said.

We made our way up, fussed Darcy, who was so pleased to see us he did the wall of death around the lounge before laying down and falling instantly asleep — short, intense bursts of exercise really whack him out.

All afternoon we sat and made plans on how we were going to raise five pounds for fuel to get us to the market on Saturday. We needed several different strategies in case one didn't work, but they pretty much all centred around selling or bartering for eggs.

The months went by and we struggled on, living on nothing. Mostly, we ducked and dived and found a way of getting by. There were days when it all flared up, and there were girly tears and tantrums, but Debbie learned to just ignore me until I calmed down.

To be fair, we both had our moments. The daily battle to survive is just so tiring, and the phone calls to companies begging for more time to pay utterly demoralising. Just when we were reaching our lowest ebb, when we really didn't think we could go on much longer, we got another phone call from Gary Rhodes' TV producer, asking if we wanted to enter the *Local Food Heroes* competition again. What the heck, the exposure last year had given us lots of publicity and a few extra orders, so we said yes. It felt like a final shot.

CHAPTER
THIRTY-EIGHT

The film crew came back, again with Michael Caines, who bundled happily into the house, made a fuss of Darcy, kissed Debbie, shook my hand and wandered up to the loo, making us feel as though he were an old friend popping by rather than a famous TV personality here for a filming.

This time, a couple of days after they'd finished, they phoned us up and said: "You've won for the South West! Congratulations!"

Then they said, can you come to the studio and take part in the grand final? There were 12 finalists in total, and they wanted each of us to cook our own dish using our own produce on camera for Gary Rhodes.

Oh, yes!

The overall winner, chosen by Gary Rhodes and a panel of esteemed food judges, would win £40,000.

Forty grand! A 1-in-12 chance of winning 40 grand — now that's the kind of odds I can work with.

I did a little jiggy dance right there and then in the lounge and realised I hadn't danced in any capacity for well over a year. Not a step in time with any music, not even anything in my head. I grabbed Debbie in a clinch and twirled her around and around. She laughed and twirled me back. "Hey, I'm supposed to be the leader here!" I complained, feeling myself being led into something between a waltz and a drunk staggering down the street.

More than anything, that moment made me think how serious we'd become. Not only had we not danced for a year, but we'd hardly laughed either. We'd probably smiled at a sitcom or a joke, but I don't mean that, I mean the laughter two people share because they're happy. It's the same with the dancing: everything had become that heavy and that morbid that we hadn't even swayed to something on the radio. Not that I'm a good dancer, I'm not, I'm appalling.

I once had a dancing lesson with Len Goodman, head judge on *Strictly* and the US version, *Dancing with the Stars*. Len and my dad were best friends for years and years before my dad died right before Len became famous. When my dad married my mum, Len was his best man, and when Len married his first wife, Cherry, my dad was his best man. At some point, one of them must have thought it a good idea for Len to give me a dancing lesson. I was 9 or 10 years old. I hated dancing, and I hated touching a girl, yuck, yuck, yuck! These days, I'm much better at touching women, even if my dancing hasn't improved.

Was it just lack of money that had made us so staid and serious? Yes. Yes, I think it was. You can pretend all you like that you don't need money, but the reality is you cannot survive without it, no matter how self-sufficient you are, and we are about as self-sufficient as it's possible to get.

272

You have to pay rent, you have to pay council tax, you have to run and fuel a car, you have to pay for broadband connection and a telephone line, the list goes on. The crazy thing is, we're probably talking an extra £50 a week. For us, that's the difference between sinking and swimming.

But the thought of £40,000!

"We need to win the final," I said, extracting myself from the dance with Debbie.

"No pressure then," Debbie said, swiping a hand down her front as though dusting it. "Any ideas?"

"We need to be different. We need to stand out."

She smiled. "First time I've ever heard you say that."

"Yeah, well, first time I've ever been in with a chance of having so much money." I went and got some paper and a pen. "We need to come up with a cunning plan. Something that's going to wow them, something —"

"No," Debbie cut in. "Let's just be us, that's what got us into the final in the first place. Let's not change anything now. Let's just do everything homemade, home reared and home grown, nothing bought . . . except salt — I wonder if there's a way of making salt? I'll look into that."

"Rustic smallholder! I like it. I'll make and polish a wooden board to present it on. And I'll cut a section of that old oak tree that came down last winter and carve it into a spoon."

The atmosphere around the place instantly changed. Suddenly, we were upbeat and jokey. I wrote about how it felt to be building up to a TV cooking competition final in my newspaper column, and had accepted more magazine article ideas from pitches I wrote in this week than ever before.

Things were good, and then things hit the toilet once again. Two days before the final, we received a letter in the post. It was from the estate agents. It was very formal and very to the point. We'd fallen a little behind on the rent, not masses, just a month or two. The letter stated that we had one week to catch up and pay in full, or accept notice to vacate.

The atmosphere around the place changed back. We both knew that this was the end of the road.

"We might as well do the final, and then . . ." I said, not finishing, but not needing to when I saw Debbie nodding.

Paula drove all the way down from London to cover us with the animals for the day. Early in the morning we loaded the truck with all the paraphernalia we'd need and set off for the huge old manor house the production company had hired for the day in which to film the final.

The journey took two-and-a-half hours. When we arrived, I was desperate for the bathroom and spotted a lady standing off to one side of a knot of people, all obviously part of the production company. I wandered over to her. "Excuse me," I said. She looked up and smiled. "Could you tell me where the toilet is, please?"

She stifled a laugh into her hand and shook her head. "No, sorry, I don't know. Maybe ask one of the others?" she suggested.

I did and I found it and made my way back to Debbie. The room in which we were all kept was plush, full of antique tables with old brass lamps on them and lots of overstuffed sofas set higgledy-piggledy, presumably to avoid any sense of formality. It had the feel of a cross between a Victorian hotel lobby and a gentlemen's club.

Gary Rhodes made his way into the room, and everyone fell silent. He made a statement about how pleased he was to see everyone, told us a little of what to expect and then introduced us to his co-judges, Mark Hicks, three-Michelin-star chef, and Allegra McEvedy, restaurateur, influential food writer and TV presenter — oh, and the person I'd asked to direct me to the lavvy.

While she was talking, I leaned over and told Debbie in a whisper.

She mouthed, "You prat!" I did one of those smiles that have no humour in them at all and are just meant for agreement.

The contestants were split in two groups, those who were to cook in the morning and those who were to cook in the afternoon. We were in the morning crew.

As only one person could cook and represent each finalist, Debbie went off to cook for us. This is her menu:

Starter

Home-cured ham hock and garden vegetable soup
Homemade soda bread with homemade butter —
served on a homemade breadboard
with a homemade oak spoon

275

Main course

Roast rolled shoulder of pork
Pink fir apple potatoes
Sweetheart cabbage with home-cured pancetta
Apple and honey sauce
Crackling on the side

While each of the contestants cooked, the judges moved from bench to bench to chat and taste, and when the time limit was up, everyone was dismissed, leaving only the judges and film crew to discuss, break down what was good, what was not so good, who they liked and who wasn't quite so brilliant.

There was a lot of waiting around.

When everyone had cooked and presented their best dishes, the judges went away to make their final choice of the top three.

Debbie was pleased with the food she'd cooked, but had we gone too far along the rustic route? It was almost peasant food she'd served, the irony of which wasn't lost on us. But it was too late to change anything now.

We'd done our best, but the threat of losing our home had cast a big black shadow over everything else, and it's hard to concentrate and be on top form with a black cloud over you.

Everyone was asked to gather around in a huge horseshoe with Gary Rhodes, Allegra McEvedy and Mark Hicks in the centre. Then they read out, in reverse order, the top three.

In third place, not us.

In second place, not us.

And in first place . . . not us.

The winners had all produced slick, polished restaurant-style food. We had gone too rustic. Miles too rustic, which is maddening because we can do fine-dining presentation, we just thought it would be better not to. Big mistake.

I watched Gary Rhodes give the award and a cheque for £40,000 to a posh fish-and-chip restaurant.

I fumbled for Debbie's hand, and when I found it, I felt her squeeze mine. There was a lot in the squeeze, a lot of understanding, a lot of pain, hurt and sadness. Our big hope was over.

Champagne was handed out, and we all toasted the winner through gritted teeth, with every one of us silently wishing the winner all the bad luck in the world. It's nothing personal, it's just jealousy.

With the cameras off and filming finished, Gary Rhodes set about mingling.

"I'm so proud of you!" I said to Debbie, cupping her face in my hands. "You were brilliant!" She looked at me with tears beginning to seep from her eyes.

"Debbie," Gary Rhodes said, moving over to us and placing his hand on her shoulder. "I just want to tell you that I'm a massive fan of yours. That food was fantastic, and I love what you do, the way you keep your animals and how you look after them. I think it's brilliant. Don't be upset by not winning. We had to pick a winner, and the person we picked was right for this programme and for today. For ages, you were in second place. Keep doing what you're doing. I think it's fantastic and very special."

He stayed for ages and gave us a pep talk — how he knew we needed one, I have no idea. He really boosted us. I watched him afterwards, and he didn't go around to any of the others and do the same thing, so I can only assume he really was genuine.

Then Allegra McEvedy sought Debbie out and said much the same thing. "I know you didn't win, though right up until the end you were in second place — I don't know what happened there. Anyway, when you watch the programme and hear our comments, I think you'll be really pleased."

"Wow, you really impressed them," I said after she'd wandered away.

"Michael Caines said much the same thing to me when he was filming," she said.

"Did he? You never told me that."

"He said our pork was as good as the pork he serves at Gidleigh Park." To even be used in the same sentence as Michael's restaurant Gidleigh Park, universally accepted as one of the top five restaurants in the world, is an honour, let alone to say our pork was as good as his! These guys are at the pinnacle of their profession and never say things for the sake of it. Nice compliment.

"Blimey."

We packed up and drove home, not exactly punching each other on the shoulder but not far from it. Okay, so we didn't win. We lost out on 40 grand, but Gary Rhodes had come over and made a point of saying he was a massive fan of Debbie's, and Michael and Allegra had both raved about us. Money issues aside, that's the sort of accolade you can't ignore.

The darkest hour is always the one before dawn. The next day, I phoned up my mum and asked if I could borrow some money. "Can I borrow some money? I won't be able to pay you back," I said. Forty years old and I was going to my mum cap in hand for some money. How embarrassing. But I was desperate, screaming desperate. I told her what it was for.

"I thought you were keen on moving back to London?" she said.

No. Not anymore. It struck me that not once in all the 10 years we'd been down here had a single person said they believed in what we were doing. Not once. Now all of the sudden we had celebrities — celebrities whom we looked up to and watched on the television — saying they not only believed in us, but they admired what we were doing. Why on earth would I want to give that up and move back?

"No, mum," I said, "we're never going to move back," and I realised, probably for the first time ever, that that was true. London would always be my first love, a place I had a huge soft spot for and thought of fondly, but I'd moved on. I was married to Exmoor now. And we had children . . .

The kittens Niko and Morris (Morris now without a tail)

Dex, the one-eyed collie dog

The General, 50 stone of porcine handsomeness

Kylie, Geraldine and sows

Piglets, adolescents and hooligans
White, the cockerel
Chickens
Ducks
Geese
Lucky-Turkey-Leaky
Georgie and Pandora, the horses
Darcy, the mummy's boy Great Dane
Sheep and lambs

"Can I borrow the money anyway, mum, please?" I begged.

CHAPTER
THIRTY-NINE

With the cheque from my mum, the threat of losing our home was removed and things returned to something like normal, but normal with a buzz about it. I felt energised and motivated. Rather than plodding, I walked briskly between the animals. I couldn't do enough for them. I spent every daylight hour fussing and being with them. I thought I was doing well. I was inspired like never before. I had ideas!

"Debbie?" I'd been calling for her and walked in to find her standing in the middle of the lounge, a foot away from the television, with tears rolling down her cheeks. I touched her face and thumbed away a couple of the runners. "What is it, what's wrong?"

"Nothing. Oh, I don't know. It's just relentless work, work, work. I never see you, and we never get a day off anymore, we never get to go out. My only social life is the farmers' markets. I used to go to restaurants. I used to do stuff . . ." She puffed out a long breath of air. "Sorry. I'll be okay tomorrow. It's just now, you know?" I nodded. "Anyway, why were you calling me?"

"It doesn't matter," but I wasn't getting away with it that easily. Sure, I could've made something up. In the circumstances, maybe I should have, but I didn't. I grinned and told her my latest idea, "I was thinking maybe we should get a cow."

Silence. Then, "Pardon?"

"Look, I know what you're thinking —"

"— oh, trust me on this, you have no idea what I'm thinking."

"But a house cow would be great. We could learn to milk her. Get one of those three-legged wooden stools — I could make one!" She rolled her eyes. "Mm, point taken, buy one then — and a metal bucket. It'll be great. Think of all the butter we could make, the cheese, the cream."

"The early mornings, the milking in the rain," she added. "You'd need a cow and calf of course, one still suckling so you could take some of the milk and leave the rest for the calf. You might even need three, cow, calf and a suckler. I'll do some research."

"Three. I don't know I want three, and how early, exactly, is early?"

"Just before dawn probably. Still, you could use the small barn opposite the house. You could milk in there."

"Me! I don't know. I wasn't thinking three cows, and I wasn't thinking early mornings. It's a big commitment. We'd have to be here every day to milk. It's okay in the summer, but in the winter? We'd go out less than we do now."

"Simon, we don't go out as it is. I could get my cheese press out. Homemade ricotta is to die for. I've always loved Jersey cows, such pretty eyes. No! A Devon Ruby, oh, they're so sweet. Perhaps we could get one in calf to a meat bull. And the excess milk we could feed to the pigs."

"Hang on, a minute ago you were crying because there's too much work to do. Now you want to get a cow and . . . how many calves?"

"Just two. And that was different. I feel better now."

"What?"

"I feel better," she shrugged. "Who do we know who keeps house cows? I'll ask around. We need to think about TB testing and passports, and we'll need to register with the British Cattle Can't-Remember-The-Next-Bit, I'll Google that, and . . . Simon, are you crying?"

"Of course I'm not! It's just, there's always so much to do. I don't know that I want more work. I don't know that I want to get up before dawn and go out milking on top of everything else."

"I know, I know . . . ooh, I know someone who knows. Look, you can name the cows, how's that? I'll go and make some calls. Hey, I love you."

She left and I went and stood in her spot in the middle of the lounge a foot away from the television and cuffed my damp eyes with the back of my sleeve just as she had.

In the end, we compromised and bought two milking goats. Goats are easier to do than cows, though you still have to milk them twice a day. I got an old chest freezer from a recycle centre and put a rubber mat on top, fixed a bucket at one end that I fill with feed and that's where I milk. Suddenly, we were home-dairying, self-sufficient in milk, cream, butter, cheese, yoghurt and ice cream. It's very satisfying, and Amber and Bee are the most annoyingly adorable goats on the planet. They follow me around like dogs and, from the outset, flouted the regulation code for new females on the farm to hate me. Instead, they were coming over, leaning against me and twisting their heads back until they were looking upside down at me with big, loving eyes. I wasn't used to this at all: a female that liked me from the outset! Was there something wrong with them? Were they ill? Maybe I should have their eyesight checked?

We thought we might be able to sell the excess milk and the products we made from it. We were still chasing this extra 50 pounds a week we needed to prevent us from slipping back into debt, and three litres of milk a day would be a big step towards it, especially if we added value by turning it into cheese and yoghurt and, of course, ice cream in the summer.

Then out of the blue, Kylie died, and the fun and the energy were sucked out of life again.

It's hard to be angry when the energy has gone. But without anger, I just feel let down, not by Kylie, by . . . who? To feel let down must mean there's someone in control.

God?

God.

I think I want there to be a God so that one day I can go and bang on His door and demand He tell me what all this is about. Why do we automatically follow the line that, when we die, we have to account to Him for *our* actions? What's wrong with me storming into His office and yelling at the top of my voice, *"Why did you take my Kylie?"*

Kylie was my best friend. I love her, and I miss her so much.

Doing the pigs now is not the same. She was the matriarch, and without her, the whole dynamic of the group has changed. They're unpredictable, and there are times when I don't even feel safe. The closeness between me and them has gone, as though she was the bridge between us.

For weeks, I didn't talk to the pigs, just went down and did what needed to be done in silence. I missed Kylie, but I also missed having a best friend. We got two more sows, Pippa and Maddy, and I thought I could become close to Pippa, but of course best friends are a two-way decision and Pippa hated me.

It was only after a while that I realised that every time I went down, the General would hang around me. We'd always got on, but I'd just assumed my best friends would always be female. Could I be best friends with a male pig? Could I be best friends with the General?

I tried it out, and between us we did all the things you do to test a person for best-friend qualities. First, we tried to see if we could sit together and be comfortable. Then we tested each other's trust and loyalty, sense of humour and outlook, and if we could be open and real with one another.

"You seem happier," Debbie commented one evening as I came in, chatting about the General and the funny things we'd done together.

"I *am* happier," I said, pouring a glass of murky-looking homemade wine — wine in the loosest sense of the word. "I'm getting on so well with the General, he's such a good lad, and he's got such a dry sense of humour. Pippa seems to have taken on the role of matriarch now, and the group seems to be sorting itself out."

"Good, because I've had an idea for making some money, and I think it's something you'll really enjoy. Why don't we start running courses? Invite people down and teach them about smallholding life, about the animals, about how to look after the chickens —"

"You know I don't like the chickens!"

She raised her eyebrows at me, and I found I couldn't keep a straight face.

"Yeah, right," she said, smiling too. "I'm serious. You could show them about pigs, we could teach them how to milk Amber, and we could show them how to humanely dispatch, pluck and draw a meat bird and make it oven ready . . ."

I still think back to that chicken that Ziggy and I killed. Just awful. One of the worst moments of my life. Maybe when I've screamed at God to tell me why He took Kylie, He'll say, I didn't think you were interested in the animals after the way you laughed when you killed that chicken. Would He have a point? I don't know. Yeah, I laughed, but it wasn't because it was funny, and I think I feel more ashamed of that moment than anything else I've ever done in my life.

Today I keep the meat birds separate from the hens. That way, I know to look after them and make sure they're happy and cared for, but not to love them too much. I've also got a humane dispatcher so the end is instant, painless, without fear, and they know nothing about it. I find I can just about live with that.

"... we could butcher and process a pig in the kitchen," she continued. "Show them how to make bacon and sausages, chorizo, ham and gammon, black pudding, hogs pudding and brawn. We could do some dairy with the milk. We could offer one-day or two-day courses. What do you think?"

I started laughing. "You really think anyone's going to be interested in what we do?"

We put a page on our website and a month later held our first course.

CHAPTER
FORTY

"Simon, where are you?"

I'm in the shower. You can hear the water running —
you must be able to hear the water running. So you
know where I am.

"Are you in the shower?"

Yes, I'm in the shower. Two minutes' peace in the
mornings, that's all I ask. Well, it's not *all* I ask, obviously.
I know I ask a lot more than that; in fact, I probably
spend all day asking for stuff. But Debbie and I are a
team, and we have our departments: mine are the animals
and the land, and hers are the kitchen and food.

"Only, I was wondering if you'd had time to make
bread this morning?"

Of course it wouldn't work if we both stuck rigidly to
our departments, so there's lots of crossing over.

"Yes, it's proving, I'll bake it when I'm done here," I
shout.

"Thank you."

You're welcome. Lathering up, I realise we're down
on everything — shampoo, soap and shaving cream.
Sometimes I wonder what it must be like to nip down
the shops and buy fresh supplies. Expensive, I should
think. Does it give you more freedom to be able to

simply buy what you want? It certainly gives you more time. I'm not immune to advertising; I watch the TV adverts of young, good-looking guys shaving or using the latest shower gel scented to draw the attention of stunning women from miles around, but I'm not jealous . . . much . . . Oh, come on, I wouldn't want to do anything, I'm in love with Debbie, but can any of us honestly put our hand on our heart and say we wouldn't want beautiful people to be attracted to us? It doesn't mean you have to jump into bed with them, just a smile would be nice.

I use the last of the rosemary shampoo and make a mental note to pick some leaves to make more shampoo tonight. While I'm at it, I might as well make soap and shaving cream. Does the smell of rosemary make girls smile, I wonder?

"You're taking ages, what are you doing in there?"

Trying to clean myself with a soap bar the size of a boiled sweet — one that's been sucked. "Nothing, sweetheart, on my way."

Of course advertising isn't directed at me, not anymore. I'm self-sufficient! Which is fine, but it's not exactly sexy. I step out of the shower and squint at myself in the mirror, can't see a thing, reach for my glasses, put them on and look properly. I imagine I'm in a TV advert, I'm the good-looking hunk — it takes a bit of imagination. I give the mirror my best smouldering look and pat my cheek the way I see them do on TV. Then I imagine Debbie with barely anything on sneaking up behind me, and maybe a couple of other girls, too — give a man a fantasy and one woman is never enough.

"Ooh," they'd chorus, "You smell *divine!* What's that you're wearing?"

"Just a little something I picked out of the herb garden, something I like to call — rosemary. You like it?"

"Like it? *Come here, tiger!*"

"Simon, who are you talking to in there?" Debbie calls through the door.

"No one. I'm on my way." I grab a towel and dash from the bathroom.

In the bedroom I pull on a pair of homemade boxer shorts, ones where the elastic still works, and find some socks without any holes in them. I look longingly at the single pair of good jeans I own, the pair reserved for farmers' markets and going out, then reach for the work jeans, the ones that are more patches than denim and have a horribly baggy bum. T-shirt, fleece over the top and I'm ready for the day.

In the kitchen the bread is now fully proved, and I place it in the oven.

"So," Debbie said from behind me, "What's the plan for today?"

"I need to do the breakfast rounds," I said. "Then can you help me move some of the pigs around?"

"No, sorry, I've got urgent stuff to do here. Can we do it tomorrow — no, hang on, tomorrow's out, too. The day after?"

"What day's that?"

"No idea," she admitted. Well, it didn't matter.

"Yeah, that's fine. I'll do the morning rounds, chop some wood for the fire and then get some bits together

290

so I can make shampoo and soap. Did you know we were nearly out?"

She thought for a second. "I did, but I don't think you're going to have time to do that today."

We went on talking about all the things we needed to do, all the things that were a little urgent, more urgent and ultra urgent, and set about compiling a list that she outlined. "You're going to go down and do the morning rounds, then come up, unless you see any mushrooms in which case pick them and bring them up with the eggs, and Amber milk. If you don't see any mushrooms, then just bring up the milk and save the eggs for tonight. I'll finish off the bread, make some butter, and, depending on mushrooms or not, I'll make lunch or breakfast. Then I can start processing, while you chop wood, it's freezing in here!" The list went on, and on, and on, and the variables only confused me. Contra to instructions, my ears stopped receiving. After an hour of drilling, she finally said, "Okay?"

I nodded. "I'll go and do the morning rounds, collect eggs, milk and mushrooms. Then we can work it out from there."

She gave me an annoyed look and I walked out. I hate these organising conversations. Makes me feel like a child. As if her things we need to do were more important than my things we need to do. It's not fair. If I weren't walking, I'd stamp my feet.

I collect Dex from the barn and make massive fusses of him before sending him up onto the back of the quad bike. Then we drive down the hill and onto the land together.

291

I switch off the bike and for a second the world is silent . . . and then I begin to hear the shuffling and moving of animals as they shift about in their beds and start getting up. Carefully, I take my prize possession out from my pocket, an MP3 player, and plug it in in one ear — only ever one ear or I wouldn't be able to hear what else is going on. There's no music on the player but an audio book. One book, that's all I've been able to afford so far. I press "Play". The book is *A Fraction of a Whole* by Steve Toltz. I'm on my 12th run-through. Sometimes I wonder how much of an influence this book is having on me, and how different I'd be if I'd chosen *My Booky Wook* or something by Jeremy Clarkson.

The first part of the morning rounds is always the worst because everyone wants to be fed and watered at the same time. I throw some food in for the first set of pigs and then let out all the chickens along with Lucky-Turkey-Leaky, then the ducks and the geese. I shout at the sheep and rattle a bucket, "Sheep, sheep! Come and get your breakfast, come and get it while it's hot."

Rattle, rattle, rattle.

"That's it, come on, you sheep. Who's the joker who ordered mint sauce with their boiled egg and soldiers? Let me tell you, chef was not impressed!" They all come diving around and I pour sheep nuts onto the grass.

Then I do the pigs.

"Good morning, ladies and gentleman, I am your waiter for today, service charge is not included in the bill, so please tip heavily. General, chef says she cannot do pizza, chips and beans for breakfast, I'm afraid.

292

Neither can she do curry." I sprinkle pig nuts into each enclosure, "So you'll have to make do with this."

Honestly, give a man a solitary life and he can make conversation with anything. You know, one day I'm probably going to discover they've been able to understand every word I've said all along. They'll say, "We wanted to know about the world, and about science, beauty and love, and all you told us were dirty jokes and teased us over food." Maybe I should read them some poetry every now and then.

I play with Dex in the field and in the woods while I search for mushrooms, but the only ones I can find have been devoured by insects. I milk Amber into a shiny silver pail — it's a good milking, two litres.

I change rugs on the horses and turn them out, muck out the stables and lay beds ready for the night, fill hay nets and top up water buckets. Last job is to feed and water the meat chickens. As I drive out and shut the gate behind me, I can see Dex in the duck house squirming tight into a corner, keeping still while the ducks and chickens, Lucky-Turkey-Leaky and geese all take turns going in and scratching about around him. That's his job, to stay down in the chicken field during the day and be with the poultry, protecting them from all predators. He really is the happiest little boy in the world.

I call, "See you later, Dex," and for a brief second he peers out at me before whipping back in place. Then I drive up the hill to the house — a house, or more precisely a kitchen, that I find couldn't be any busier if an entire Women's Institute branch had descended and rolled up their sleeves for work.

All four hobs are on with saucepans simmering and steam rising, there's a food processor whirring, a mincer mincing, several bowls with wooden spoons poking out of them and the oven is on full blast. There are jars on the side waiting to be filled, and some already brimming and cooling down. The radio is on *and* the television. And in the centre, looking frazzled as though she's only just keeping up, is Debbie.

"Where have you been?" she demands.

I find a space on the table and put Amber milk down.

"Don't be like that," I say, wondering if there's a chance of a coffee anytime soon.

"Eggs?" she says, looking at my empty hands.

"There weren't any mushrooms, so you told me to leave the eggs until tonight."

"No, I need eggs."

She needs eggs. Great. "I will run down and get them for you, my little piranha fish."

"Don't be arsy."

"Well, don't be arsy with me! You told me not to worry about the mushrooms if there weren't any eggs."

"Other way around."

"What?"

"I told you not to worry about the eggs if you couldn't find any mushrooms. You said —"

"Oh, for fuck's sake!"

On that rather touching exchange, I storm out.

CHAPTER
FORTY-ONE

We've started arguing a lot. Crazy thing is, money problems are now pretty much manageable. We're getting one or two courses booked a month, and while we don't have any spare cash, we can at least meet the bills most of the time. Provided nothing unexpected comes in.

We're rowing because we're tired, and we're tired because we're now self-sufficient in just about everything. You can't believe how much time it takes doing things yourself. If we went without sleep and worked 24 hours a day, flat out, we still wouldn't get everything done. Simple things like making soap takes half a day — damn, if I don't make soap today, I'll have to resort to cutting a lemon in half and using that, though you do have to remember to dilute before tackling any sensitive areas, a mistake you would assume one would only ever make once, but no, one did it twice, on consecutive days. One can be an utter eejit.

The animals take about seven hours each day, Debbie's cooking and processing 12 to 14 hours a day. Tending the vegetable garden, one to two hours a day. In addition, I have to write if there's a magazine or

newspaper deadline looming, and then there's mainten-
ance on the land, getting ready for farmers' markets,
making bread, making butter, the list goes on and on.
Part of the problem is that it always feels as though
we're reacting to the most urgent things all the time,
never having the chance to be proactive — meaning, we
never feel as though we're making any headway. It's
frustrating. Amber milk builds up, you have to process
it. Eggs build up, you have to process them. A pig needs
to go, you have to process it. We fancy chicken, I have
to pluck and draw it. Too many tomatoes, process.
Runner beans, process. Logs — oh, logs! Half an hour
minimum every day chopping logs.

There's not enough time to do the things that need
to be done, let alone the things that we would *like* to
get done. We've had one holiday in all the 10 years
we've been living down here. I can't remember the last
time we had a barbecue and sat around relaxing: three,
maybe four years ago?

I collected 11 eggs from the nest boxes, then made
my way back up to the house. I'd been gone maybe 10
minutes, which, it seems, is enough time to shut
everything down. The kitchen was dark and silent.
Everything was turned off. I found Debbie sitting in the
lounge wiping tears from her eyes. I sat down next to
her.

"I am so tired I feel sick," she said. I put my arm
around her and she snuggled in.

I said, "I got the eggs."

She nodded. "I don't want us to keep arguing. I hate
it when we fight. We're too busy, we're too tired, I can't

think straight. I don't know that I can go on like this. Self-sufficiency is just too time consuming; everything just takes so long! It's too much."

"Why does everything take so long?"

"Because it does."

"No, seriously," I urged, "Why does it take so long?"

"Because that's how it's done."

"Can't we cheat?" I hadn't formulated this as a thought, but now that I said it, it began to dawn on me how precise, accurate and authentic we were trying to be. "We're trying to be too precise, accurate and authentic," I said. "Most of these old ways are exactly that — old ways, thought up and practised before modern gadgets and ingredients were invented. We must be able to cut some corners. Not with the animals maybe, but certainly with the processing, preserving and everything else."

It was a good argument: after all, we were following methods and recipes that were one or two hundred years old, and we were following them to the letter. "If anyone can duck and dive, it's us," I continued. "We're from London, the home of ducking and diving. We're streetwise. We're canny."

Debbie fell silent for a while, then said, "You know, you might be on to something? I'm sure I can strip down some of the recipes — God, what a fool I've been. Trying to do everything so correctly. You're right, we've got to use a bit of London savvy. All this time I've tried so hard to leave London behind, and that's the one thing I should have been embracing. We are streetwise. We can duck and dive. We just need to incorporate some of that into what we're doing here. Who cares if we make butter the old-fashioned way or a new, quicker way of our own invention as long as we end up with butter?"

I left her napping on the sofa while I cleared up the kitchen. So we are going to bring a bit of London attitude into our world. A bit of "We can do that, but we can do that *our* way". Strip down all the recipes and everything and streamline it. Modernise it. Make it easy — three days to make brawn and we charge a pound a slice at the farmers' market? Are we insane? I bet we could make brawn in a couple of hours if we thought about it and tweaked the recipe. Some things we wouldn't be able to cut down on, things like chopping logs, but if we could cut in half the time we spend on half the things we do, then we'll save a quarter of our day. Blimey.

For the next two weeks, we spent night after night on the Internet and took ideas from people all over the world. Reading blogs and joining forums are fantastic because people post what they're doing. You might get a tip from a girl living in the hills of Spain, and another from a sheep farmer in New Zealand, and you just adapt them to your own environment and circumstances. There really are some clever people on the Internet with exceptional ideas.

Mostly, we just updated and modernised everything we were doing. Brought it into the modern day. If the recipe said "do everything in stages", we altered it so we could do it all in one. If it said 'thicken by reducing', we added cornflour instead. When you start looking at what you're doing and search for short cuts, it's amazing how much faff you can cut out. Even making things like Cheddar cheese (the recognised way gives you this long and involved process that takes hours) you can do in virtually one go. Okay, so it's not *authentic* and purists would have the urge to burn me at the stake, but unless we found a way of cutting back on the time we spent working, self-sufficiency was going to drag us under. We took self-sufficiency and we used a streetwise city attitude to give it a makeover.

Things became fun again. We were achieving the same level of output as before, but in a fraction of the time, which meant we weren't as tired. Which meant we didn't argue anywhere near as much.

I thought, I could write a book about this, about how to become self-sufficient. But it's impossible to get a book published. Absolutely impossible. Not worth the effort of trying. Then again, what's the harm in giving it a go? I contacted an agent, who contacted a publisher, who commissioned me to write *The Self Sufficiency Bible — from window boxes to smallholdings, hundreds of ways to become self-sufficient.*

Well, maybe it wasn't quite that simple. Truth is, I'd been knocking on the door of agents up and down the country for years with nothing to show but heaps of rejections. But now I had something strong and different to offer, and I was taken on. City boy to farmer is one thing, but estate agent to author, now that's a leap that's seldom made. With the spare time I'd created in our day, I settled down and wrote the book.

Things were going so well that when Debbie's birthday came up, I gave her the choice: we could either go out for a nice little pub lunch (yeah, things were going *that* well — we hadn't been out to a pub for lunch for about . . . well, since my brother and mother were down), or I could buy her 20 ex-battery hens. She chose the hens. I saved up and we did both.

Battery hens. Just for a moment imagine you have never been outside. Not only have you never *been* outside, but you have never even *seen* outside. As far as you know, the entire world consists of one big room packed tight with others just like you, each of you in a cage, with just about enough room to turn around. The light stays on for around 20 hours a day. It's all you know. It's all you ever *have* known . . .

That's the life for a battery hen.

We had a lovely lunch at a local pub, then we went and collected the 20 hens, packed them into special poultry crates and slid them into the back of the truck. They were a bit bedraggled, most had feathers missing, especially around their necks where they would have poked their heads out through the bars of the cage to try and look around, and all of their combs were pale and flat. Other than that they just looked sad.

I carefully drove back to the smallholding, bumped down our track and pulled up beside their new home. I had adapted an old shed by cutting off the bottom two feet all the way around so it sat more squat and the chickens would be able to see out the windows. I had fixed some perches inside and covered the entire thing in chicken wire for protection.

300

As carefully as I could, I placed each chicken inside the shed. There was water, feed and light from the windows, and it looked fab (at least I thought it did). To them, it looked scary as hell. As I placed each one down, they ran into the darkest corner until they were all huddled in a clump. With nothing more I could do except give them time and space to explore and get used to their new environment, I shut the door and left them in peace.

I made a fuss of Debbie all afternoon, and we didn't return for a couple of hours. When we did, we peeked in and saw all of them standing in a straight line staring goggled-eyed out of the windows. The shed is smack bang in the centre of the chicken field with its trees, rushes, long grass areas and short grass, all with happy chickens and poultry going about their business. I would love to have let them out there and then, but felt it would be all too much for them, so we left them overnight to get used to the sights and sounds.

In the morning, armed with hot coffee and set for a couple of hours' watching, we opened the doors on the chickens for the first time in their little lives. There was no rush. In fact, for ages none of them ventured any closer than the threshold, where every now and then one would stick their head out, peck the grass and then go running back inside. But little by little, they got bolder until the first one hopped out and landed on the springy grass.

With one out, a few more followed. Then a few more, until they were all out — and then it started raining. As soon as the first droplets hit the ground, they all dashed back inside and had a long, loud chat about what was happening. It was lovely to see their adventure. After 15 months of living in a horrible battery unit, it felt like today was the first real day of their lives and it was wonderful to be part of it.

"That was a really lovely thing to do," Debbie said, taking my arm and resting her head on my shoulder. "It makes me feel nice that we rescued some chickens for my birthday rather than buying a present, and I loved going out for lunch."

Rain started falling quite hard. "We've probably got enough chickens to justify another cockerel now," I said. "If we still had Red, it wouldn't be an issue, but I'm not sure White is up to the challenge of humping 50 women a day. He's struggling with the group he's got, let alone adding these to his daily 'to do' list. I wonder how they'll react when we put in a male with them? They'll have never seen a man before. Poor things. We'd better get a youngster, they're likely to wear the poor bugger out."

CHAPTER
FORTY-TWO

In the same newspaper as my column, someone had advertised a Jersey Giant cockerel free to a good home. We went and picked him up. He was *huge*, and so beautifully black, that deep, rich black, that in the sun he almost looks green. He was stunning. Very proud. A true cockerel's cockerel. We put him in with the hens, and collectively they took one look at him and melted. It was *Sex and the City* poultry style. I could almost see the thoughts flitting through their minds.

"He's so big . . ."

"And so hunky . . ."

"And so manly . . ."

"And so handsome . . ."

"And so horny . . ."

"And I *so* want to be first . . ."

They sidled up to him, cooed and fluttered their eyelids. He stood there, absorbing the attention and growing taller with each new woman that approached.

"What shall we call him?" Debbie asked.

"We can't call him Black because when the sun shines, he's got hundreds of different shades of green in him. Look at him . . ." The longer he stood in one place, the more women he collected. All the other hens, the ones from White, were now joining his harem. "For the first time in my life, I'm jealous of a chicken."

She hit me. Then said, "What about Red?"

"Oh yeah! Okay, the second time," and she hit me again. I smiled. So did she. "It's official: the coolest man on the farm is now a cockerel."

He was trying to walk, but with a carpet of women around him was making slow progress.

I watched and said, "He's like a surf dude walking down the beach collecting women — Dude! We could call him Dude!"

Debbie groaned.

"Look at him, he *is* such a Dude," I said. "It's perfect."

I left Debbie watching over Dude and his girls, put a bag of feed on the back of the quad and drove down to do the evening rounds of the pigs. At the end of the path, I coasted down the short hill to the gate. I unlatched the gate, and as I was turning to go back to the bike, a pig-shaped splodge out of place caught my eye. It was on the path further down. I leaned on the gate and peered closer. Had someone escaped? It wasn't moving, and you would expect an escapee to be running up and down showing off to all the others. Was it ill? Then two things hit me at once. The first was the realisation that the pig-shaped splodge was nothing more than a water bucket that had been tossed over the fence line and was resting at an odd angle to make it look a little like a pig. The second thing to hit me was my quad bike.

As I'd been standing trying to work out what the splodge was, the bike had begun rolling down the small incline towards me. I felt a gentle push on the back of my legs, and would have stepped away, but where I'd been standing I'd sunk a little into the mud and the suction was just enough to prevent me stepping off. Instead, the momentum of the bike pushed me forward. Unable to move my feet, I went down onto my knees.

Above me, the bike kept coming. There's just no loyalty from farm machinery. Frantic, I tried to scrabble out from underneath it, but the mud was wet and cloying, and I couldn't get a purchase. I was on all fours and could sense the bike rolling further and further over the top of me. Luckily, I'd been standing straight in front of it so the wheels were rolling either side of my shins and not touching me at all. But that's little consolation when you're running yourself over with your own vehicle. Safety is way down the list. Feeling like a prat is much higher. I thought, this is just perfect, just . . . *perfect*! Then the bike hit me in the bum and sent me sprawling headfirst into the mud.

Slowly, slowly, slowly — we don't want to rush the humiliation now — the bike inched its way up and over my thighs, the tires still either side of me, engine chugging, making its way up my legs until the underside hit my bottom, where it came to rest. Thank God for a big bottom. Yeah, I bet they don't teach that at Weight Watchers: slim down and you'll never stop an escaping quad bike from running you over. Big bums are for safety!

Nothing of the bike was touching me bar a light pressure on my derriére, but it was enough. I was stuck. Stuck fast, the mud preventing me from moving beneath, and the bike preventing me from moving above. Humiliation was complete.

I lay still. Well, there wasn't a lot else I could do. Debbie would come and find me soon. I closed my eyes and winced at the thought. I imagined her rushing up, her face full of worry. I pictured myself twisting so I could look up at her and smile. "Oh, hello, dear, don't be alarmed. Risk assessment. Just checking to see if it's possible to run yourself over with your own vehicle, and it seems it is. So there you go. Job done. Ha-ha, health and safety gone mad in this country. Still, better safe than sorry. Now we know. Well, I think that just about covers it. If you could be a pet and reverse the bike off me, that would be great."

I closed my eyes and let my face flop into the wet mud.

CHAPTER
FORTY-THREE

From time to time, we all ask *big* questions, *life* questions: Am I happy? Do I love and feel loved by the person I'm with? Do I feel appreciated? Am I even necessary — who doesn't play *It's a wonderful life* in their head every now and then with themselves as the main character? You know the questions. They're the same for all of us.

It's been a year since I ran myself over with the quad bike. That makes it nearly 11 years since we left London. Eleven years from the time that I got drunk in a North Devon pub with an elderly jazz band playing in the corner and ballroom-dancing farmers waltzing on the dance floor. Eleven years since I agreed to change my life forever.

I've kicked and screamed against it; that's only natural. But I've worked hard, too. Of course there's no way of knowing how I would have answered the *big* questions had we not made the change and moved away, no way of knowing how our life would have progressed. Would I have remained an estate agent? Probably. I'd certainly have remained in London, and I'd be eating Big Macs, and I'd have, oh damn it, I can never remember what they're called . . . er, what's the name again? It folds . . . you keep it in your pocket . . . *money*! Yeah, I remember money. Lovely, lovely money. I'd be living in London and I'd have money.

But I didn't. I moved away to Exmoor and learned to talk to pigs — talk to pigs, blimey, that sounds weird even to me. No money and my best friends are pigs. Is my mother proud of me? I don't know. I'm afraid to ask.

But I know how I'd answer the *big* questions today. Weird or not, broke or not, the answers are all *yes*. In spite of myself, I've found happiness and found the spot in life where I feel most comfortable, which pretty much is sitting on the General's bum while he lays down in his bed or a mud wallow, laughing and chatting all day long to him, and nobody is more surprised at that than me.

In the last year since I ran myself over, there have been some changes you should know about. Geraldine, the wild boar, had to be put to sleep; Pandora died of old age; Dude, White and all the hens, including the ex-battery hens, were killed one night by a stoat attack; and Lucky-Turkey-Leaky passed away in her sleep. I hate it when they go, but I don't scream at God the way I used to, and I don't have the urge to storm into His office and demand answers. Things die, we lose our friends, that's life. It's sad and I don't forget them, I *never* forget them, but it's what happens.

In place of Pandora we now have an Alfie, another boy on the smallholding. He's a real feisty pony that we rescued from being sold and turned into dog meat (honest). He's had a tough life, and he's as hard and streetwise as any London teenager. The plan is to put him to a cart and use him for short trips out to the shops and for moving things around the land. We need to make a cart first, though.

So this is where we stand right now:

Darcy, the mummy's boy Great Dane
Dex, the one-eyed collie dog
Georgie and Alfie, the horses
Niko and Morris, the kittens
Amber and Bee, the goats
The General
Sows: Pippa and Maddy, Whinny and Pru
Piglets of various ages
Pukka, an Indian Game cockerel
Chickens (including another set of ex-battery hens)
Ducks
Terrorist geese
Sheep and lambs
Meat birds

Is it possible to make a cart for a horse? It must be. Pre-car, that's what everyone would have done. I wonder if you'd need an MOT? One thing's for sure: I'd never get another parking ticket — where would they stick it, on Alfie's head? But I'm never likely to get a speeding ticket either. Speed would be a thing of the past.

We still have the quad bike and the truck, too. I couldn't expect Alfie to trot the 20 miles to the feed store for all the animal food and then trot back, though the truck's not exactly Speedy Gonzales itself, so maybe speed is a thing of the past anyway.

Does that bother me? Sometimes I look at my brother's Porsche, I look at new cars on the road or I watch car programmes on TV, and I want to put my foot down in something that can go really fast, feel that blast of G-force as I get sucked into the back of my seat. I've managed to incorporate a lot of London into what we do, but there's no way of incorporating speed. Even my broadband connection out here has all the oomph of a comatosed donkey.

Funnily enough, the one thing that has turned out to be quite quick is our version of self-sufficiency: the all-new, de-faffed, streamlined and modernised do-it-yourself lifestyle. No more running out of soap and cutting a lemon in half, we're *organised*! Organised to the point of being slick. I guess in the end all lifestyles have one thing in common: you get them done as quickly as possible so you have more time left to lounge on the sofa reading a book or watching telly.

One day it would be nice if we could lounge on a sofa watching telly in our own house, maybe build one on the land — not me build one, obviously! Okay, I'll rephrase that: one day it would be nice if we could employ someone who knows what they're doing to build a house for us. One made of wood or maybe even straw — seriously, straw houses are fantastic, just loads of bales piled on top of one another between wooden struts and then plastered over. Very warm, and because they're packed so tight, you don't get any creepy-crawlies or nasties in the walls, which was the first thing I thought of.

I'd make the house cozy and normal inside with a lovely handmade wooden kitchen and modern bathroom, electricity, a comforting open fire and rugs on the floor. From the outside it would look like a cute little cottage in the woods. That's the cheap option. The expensive option is to buy a flat-packed wooden Scandinavian lodge and erect that. But for now we're still in the same house we rented 11 years ago, the one I told Debbie we'd only rent for six months to see how it went.

But builders charge money — not even my chickens could squeeze out enough eggs to barter for building a house — and that means saving up, which is always going to be a nightmare. I still have my weekly newspaper column, I write for magazines, and I even have a monthly self-sufficiency spot on BBC Radio Devon. We do farmers' markets and sell produce, and the courses have gone off the scale with enquiries coming in most days. The money from all of that just about covers the bills, the animal feed and care, and a little for us. But there's never anything left over at the end of the month to save.

"There's never anything left over at the end of the month to save," I said. Debbie gave me a what-are-you-talking-about look. "Sorry, I was just thinking out loud."

"Don't start, not tonight, please not tonight. I'm too tired," she begged.

I wasn't going to. The fire was loaded with logs and blazing away, the dog comfortably stretched out on the sofa next to Debbie, and I was uncomfortably stretched out on the floor in front of them. A nice night. I sipped some latest concoction we laughingly call wine and grimaced.

"A few more sips and the sharp edge dulls," Debbie advised. I took another sip. It wasn't any duller. In fact, two sips in quick succession made me want to whack the top of my head.

When I could speak again, I said, "One day, we'll build a house on the land, it's the next step." The fire crackled. "A simple little house in a clearing in the woods, that's our future."

"Won't that be a bit creepy at night?"

"Not at all. It would be lovely and romantic, a real pretty little cottage, a happy cottage, not a dark and dingy cottage. We'd be closer to the animals."

"You'd be closer to the General, you mean."

I made a show of thinking about it. "Well, there is that, I suppose."

"Sweetheart, you know we're running low on wood for the fire, don't you?"

Good change of subject. "Yes," I said.

"Will you be able to cut some more tomorrow?"

My life is cutting bloody wood. The fire has a bigger appetite than the animals. "So, Simon, nice to meet you, what do you do for a living?" "I cut wood." "A tree surgeon?" "No, I just cut wood. Wood, wood, wood. And collect eggs."

At times like this I miss London. I've no outlet for anger down here, no release, no *channel to send it down*. I can't display it to Debbie, she wouldn't understand, and so I end up doing these internal rants.

Whereas in London, non-violent anger where you get yourself all fired up inside is good, especially in business. To see an estate agent passionate, focused and galvanised into action is a wonderful sight.

I put another log on the fire, then another, then another, then another.

"Simon!"

I took the last one off.

The General understands, he knows what I'm talking about; at least he should, I tell him often enough.

CHAPTER
FORTY-FOUR

The next morning I did the animal rounds and got everyone up and ready for the day. Then I took my chainsaw, sharpened the blade, put on a safety hat and safety gloves and went off into the woods to find firewood.

Halfway in I stopped, took off all the kit, put down the chainsaw and walked back, calling the chickens, the goats, the sheep, the geese, the ducks and Dex, my dog, who had all decided I was about to do something really exciting and they just had to follow me to see what it was. Soppy animals and falling trees aren't exactly a match made in heaven, which, incidentally, I told them as we made our way back, is where they'd end up if they didn't stay out of the woods. Sometimes it's necessary to be harsh to be kind.

The tree I wanted was a medium-aged ash tree that was growing out of the hillside at an odd angle. It wasn't going up, as trees should, but growing out sideways. I stood looking at the tree for a long time. Cutting down trees is always dangerous work, but on this occasion, what could possibly go wrong? All I had to do was start cutting. Gravity would do the rest and pull it the short distance to the ground. Simple.

314

Standing beside the tree, I started the chainsaw. I looked out at the top where the branches ended, then followed the trunk with my eyes all the way down to the base. Nothing could go wrong. I took a stance, placed the blade on the back of the trunk and started cutting, wood shavings teeming over my legs and covering my feet. As I reached about halfway through, the tree lurched. I stopped. The half that was cut seemed to be twisting away from the half that was still attached. I looked out at the top of the tree again. Now I came to think of it, it did have more branches on one side than the other. Still, gravity is gravity. Its job is to pull things straight down, that's what it does. I went back to cutting.

The tree lurched further, the twist more pronounced now. But I was committed and carried on. Suddenly, the trunk snapped, and I watched in horror as the whole trunk locked out at me, really kicked out at me. The extra weight on one side had acted like a counterweight and twisted the entire tree, whiplashing the base out in my direction.

I put up my hand, but I might as well have been putting out my hand to a moving train. The power was awesome. It hit me on the hip and kept coming, flinging me backward, ripping the chainsaw out of my hands and tossing it away to one side.

My head hit something immovable, probably another tree. Even with the safety hat on, it was still one hell of an impact. My eyes switched off and everything went black.

I didn't have time to be scared, I didn't have time to be anything. I didn't even know if I was on the ground or still falling. I'd lost all sense, except one: the knowledge that wherever I landed, that mighty trunk, that heavy, heavy cut tree trunk was still moving and following right behind me. I waited for the impact. I thought, this is it, this is the moment of my death, splattered by a falling tree, a falling tree that I had cut down. I felt incensed that my eyes weren't working, that I couldn't watch the wooden execution as it fell. And then I thought, no, sod that, I'm glad my eyes aren't working. Who wants to watch something heavy fall on them? That's terrifying, I'd rather see blackness than that. So I watched the blackness and I waited a tenth of a second, a second, a week, a year, a lifetime. Then even that sense, the sense of waiting, left me, and I blacked out completely.

But I didn't die. Instead, I woke from the outside in, which is the opposite to how I normally wake, which is inside out so my brain starts functioning before my skin. That's the normal way to wake. It's much more difficult to have your skin wake before your brain, and much more unnerving. When my brain finally dragged itself out of the fog and into consciousness, my skin was already searching for damage. By some miracle, it didn't find any.

The tree had pushed me far enough away that I was out of reach. I opened my eyes, saw the trunk lying next to me and shivered.

"I think I might have knocked myself out," I told Debbie up at the house.

"Oh, my God. Don't go to sleep."

"I don't want to go to sleep."

"Good. That's good. Sit down. No, don't sit down, walk around. Yes, walk around. I need to get you to hospital."

I started walking with her prodding fingers into my back to keep me moving. "You haven't even asked me what happened," I said.

"You chopped a tree down on yourself," she said simply. I hate it when she does her witchy stuff.

"No, I didn't. I chopped a tree down, it kicked me, I fell over, my head hit something, and everything went blank. Then I woke up. I don't know how long I was out. It might only have been a second or two."

She stopped prodding. "The tree kicked you?"

I nodded and told her it was a long story, which it wasn't, but telling someone it's a long story is a way of saying you don't want to share. She put me in the truck and drove me to hospital. I moaned all the way that I felt fine and only ached a bit.

"Headache! Oh my God," she said, putting down her foot so we went ever faster.

"No, not a headache, my arms and my back from where I fell. My head's fine, please slow down before you kill us."

She slowed down a touch, but we still made the trip in record time. I walked into A&E for the second time since leaving London, which is the same as saying the second time in my life — there's just no danger when you're an estate agent, other than vendors angry that you haven't sold their property fast enough, and even then it seldom resorts to a level where hospitalisation might be necessary. I told the nurse what happened, and she rushed me into a cubicle.

They did tests and checks and deemed my noggin satisfactory. I was free to go, though they advised me to take it easy for a few days and added that it probably wasn't advisable to chop down trees on my own without someone else present and that I should be careful.

As if I'm not careful! What do they think: I wander along willy-nilly and go, oh yeah, look, tree, chainsaw, cut, way-hey, let's see what happens! Come on, do I look that stupid? I take time to consider the parameters of what I'm about to take on. Study the structure of the tree. Consider where it's most likely to fall. Think about the wind and other conditions that might have an impact. Then I cut it, and I don't say way-hey either. Not most of the time.

"You need rest and recuperation," Debbie said, helping me out of the car once we pulled up outside our house.

"Get off me, I'm not done in yet, you know," I said, waving her away and getting out myself. "Besides, I can't take time off. Who's going to do the animals? Who's going to look after the farm?"

On cue, the front door opened and a smiley voice said, "How's the lumberjack? Chopping a tree down on your own head, honestly, it's the height of carelessness — did you remember to change your pants before you went to hospital? I knew a nurse once . . . actually, I knew several, some of them at the same time, only this

318

one told me they hate patients with dirty pants on. I dropped everything and came as soon as I put the phone down to you, Debbie. Oh, I found some wine in the fridge and helped myself. It nearly killed me! Man, it's disgusting. So I went and bought some. Would you like a glass?"

Ziggy.

I groaned loudly. Do I groan a lot, I mean more than other people? It's difficult to know where your own groan level is in comparison because nobody ever talks about it. No one says, "Oh, I groaned six times today." I don't want to be a groaner, I don't want to have become someone who can't hold in his emotions and has to groan so other people know how he feels. Letting out emotions are good, of course, everyone loves a man who cries, but a man who groans? "Oh, my boyfriend's so cute, he groans all the time, groans at the drop of a hat." Aaahh. Maybe I'm not that bad, maybe nobody else has noticed my groans.

"I have," Ziggy said, meeting me at the front door and, unsure if he should shake my hand in case it might fall off, stepped back and waved me in.

"So have I," Debbie added, "And yes, you do groan too much. It's off-putting."

"That wasn't meant to come out," I said, putting a thank-you hand on Ziggy's shoulder and making my way past him and into the house. "Sorry. When I get stressed, the filter between my brain and my mouth stops working and the connection is direct. I'm glad you're here, thanks, Ziggy. I just hate feeling useless."

319

"Simon, of everyone I know, you, above all others should be used to it. How many years were you an estate agent?" Ziggy said.

"I don't mean useless in that sense. I mean the aftermath of the near-death experiences, this bit," I waved my hand. "I hate feeling useless and having to call on other people to help out, while I doss on the sofa to get better."

"You don't have to doss on the sofa," Debbie said, coming in behind me.

I smiled, "Oh yes, I do," and made a beeline for the lounge.

I took it easy for a couple of days. Ziggy's great, and as much as I moan (and groan) about him, I wouldn't have been able to survive without his friendship or his help. That's why on the fourth day when he suggested we all go down and sleep on the land for his last night, we reluctantly agreed.

"We'll have quilts, covers, pillows and everything, it'll be great!" he enthused. He used to be very big on the scouts. "I can't believe you've had the land for all this time and you haven't slept on it once. That would be the first thing I'd do."

"Yeah, well, you're odd. We've got a perfectly good house and you want to sleep outside on the grass?"

We took down bedding, plastic ground sheets and top covers, lit a huge bonfire and tossed a haunch of venison wrapped in tin foil into the flames. When it was ready, we cut chunks off it with pen knives and ate it with hunks of fresh, warm bread and homemade butter.

320

"I never knew if you were kidding all those times you said you would rather be back in London," Ziggy said.

I looked at Debbie. "Is he talking about you?"

She rolled her eyes.

I smiled. The fire was burning some amazing colours, reds and oranges and yellows, all dancing and leaping in the darkness, with the three of us grouped around it fully clothed underneath our separate covers. "I don't know. At times like this I wonder if I really did. It does seem a bit crazy. Does anyone want me to tell a ghost story?"

"No!" Debbie shouted.

"Would you go back?" Ziggy pressed.

"To London? No. Not in a million. This is my life now."

"Happy as pigs in shit."

"Ziggy!" Debbie said.

He laughed. "Okay, happy as pigs in clover."

Something hit my makeshift bed. I looked down. It was a pen, a cheap plastic pen. "Who threw a pen at me, Ziggy?" I said, reaching out and picking it up. It felt okay in my hand, but nothing special. The sense of comfort it used to give me wasn't there anymore, so I tossed it into the fire.

"I never thought I'd see the day," Debbie laughed.

"You threw it, didn't you? It wasn't Ziggy at all."

"Why would I have thrown a pen at you?" Ziggy said.

We were drinking wine from plastic beakers, shop-bought red wine. It was gorgeous. We talked, we laughed, and we talked some more, right into the small hours of the very dark night.

"I'm tired and drunk," Ziggy moaned.

"Me too."

"I need sleep," Ziggy moaned. "Night, Debbie."

"Night, Ziggy. Night, Simon," Debbie said.

"Night, Debbie. Night, Ziggy."

"Night, Simon."

I stared at the stars. There were a lot of stars, gazillions of them. "Night, Dex," I called. "Night, General. Night, Pippa and Maddy. Night, chickens. Night, sheep. Night, Niko: Night, Amber and Bee. Night —"

Debbie and Ziggy sat up from opposite sides of the fire and simultaneously shouted: "Shut up!"